STO

ACPL ITEM DISCARDED

S0-BWW-237

643.7 K86f
Kramer, Jack
Finishing touches

AUG 4 '78

FINISHING TOUCHES

HANDMADE INEXPENSIVE WAYS TO MAKE A HOUSE A HOME

HANDMADE
INEXPENSIVE WAYS
TO MAKE
A HOUSE A HOME

FINISHING TOUCHES

JACK KRAMER

Drawings by Adrian Martinez

McGRAW-HILL BOOK COMPANY
NEW YORK   ST. LOUIS   SAN FRANCISCO
TORONTO   DUSSELDORF   MEXICO

Books by Jack Kramer
1000 BEAUTIFUL HOUSEPLANTS AND HOW TO GROW THEM
YOUR HOMEMADE GREENHOUSE
SILHOUETTES
100 GARDEN PLANS
ESCAROLE IN THE BEDROOM
HOW TO IDENTIFY AND CARE FOR HOUSEPLANTS
ORCHIDS
CACTI AND OTHER SUCCULENTS
YOUR TRELLIS GARDEN AND HOW TO BUILD IT

Book design by Stanley Drate.

Copyright © 1978, by Jack Kramer. All Rights Reserved.
Printed in the United States of America. No part of this
publication may be reproduced, stored in a retrieval system,
or transmitted, in any form or by any means, electronic,
mechanical, photocopying, recording, or otherwise, without
the prior written permission of the publisher.

1 2 3 4 5 6 7 8 9 0   DO DO   7 8 3 2 1 0 9 8

Library of Congress Cataloging in Publication Data

Kramer, Jack, 1927-
  Finishing touches.

  Includes index.
  1. Dwelling—Remodeling. I. Title.
TH4816.K75   643'.7   77-17924
ISBN 0-07-035393-X

All photographs by Mary K. Martinez and Matthew Barr, unless otherwise specified.

CONTENTS

2011954

AUTHOR'S NOTE

This book was started when my illustrator, Adrian Martinez, purchased a twenty-year-old tract house at little cost. It was in almost impossible condition but the basic construction was there. It needed window and door treatment, wall work and new floors. It needed ceiling work and a new entrance. In essence it needed remodeling. The house was approached with an aesthetic eye and an artist's touch. This book is in most part a chronicle of that house and how it became a home. (Other remodeling details are from my own home).

My heartiest thanks to Adrian and Mary Martinez for allowing me to use their dwelling as an example of how to make a house a home for little cost and some work.

Jack Kramer

Introduction:
Get That Old-Time Feeling

Today's houses lack the charm and beauty of yesterday. Gone are the circular window, the carved moldings, the hardwood floors. Gone are the craftsmen. What we have today is the unionized carpenter and worker whose wages do not allow such amenities. Yet it is the detailing that makes the home. And *you* can add that detailing whether you have a new house or an old one.

The proliferation of handmade houses has been the answer to today's mechanization. Not everyone can build his own house but almost anyone can do something to add the beauty of yesterday, the craftsmanship we all admire. The sterile entranceway can be made inviting by using an arbor or archway. The front door, usually bland, can be handcarved or contain stained glass. And there are attractive replacements for the plain motel windows that plague so many houses. Finally, those tired floors can be redone in parquet or hardwood to give a house character. And don't forget the old-fashioned sun porch—added to a home it creates a feeling of old beauty (an ordinary porch, too, can be converted into a sun porch). The material cost is not exorbitant; the labor is. But if you do it yourself, you can afford it. There are many important remodeling touches that will make a new home stellar or an old one regain its charm.

Forget the savings (they will be ample), and consider the enjoyment of doing it yourself. There is great satisfaction in knowing you have created something beautiful and lasting. Making your home an inviting, handsome one is within your reach; with this book in hand and with over 100 drawings and photographs you can make your house what you want. So, whether you have an old or a new home that lacks the craftsman's touch, this book is for you.

Wood 1

Wood, in one form or another, can transform an ordinary house into an exceptional one. Casement windows, paneled doors, and a beamed ceiling all provide that enduring and desirable old-world charm we are always looking for. Thus some general knowledge of wood is necessary—we all know that the wood we use in building is essentially from tree trunks, but just how that tree becomes part of your house deserves attention. If you have seen a television or movie short on how wood is cut and milled and prepared for our use, you probably do not have to read this, but if you have not, by all means read on.

The bark is the coating that protects the living cells of the tree. New wood cells grow in what is called the cambium layer. Sapwood is a combination of dead and living cells and carries sap through the tree to the leaves. Sapwood is not yet fully developed wood. Heartwood is old sapwood that no longer carries or stores sap. The chemical changes that have taken place in heartwood make it stronger and heavier than sapwood. The chemicals in sapwood or heartwood determine the wood's color, resistance to decay, and odor.

The term *grain* is derived from the long cells (rings) that grow parallel to the trunk. Wood cut along or with the grain, that is, cut in the direction the cells are growing, is ten times stronger than wood cut against or perpendicular to the grain. Wood sawed tangent to the growth rings is cut with the grain; wood sawed perpendicular to the rings is cut against the grain. Plain-sawed wood—most wood is sawed this way in mills—creates a more beautiful ring pattern, costs less, and has round and small knots, thus affecting the strength of the board. Quarter-sawed wood shrinks less, twists less, and weathers better, but this method of sawing costs more than plain sawing.

Greenwood is not dried or seasoned. Seasoned wood (also called kiln-dried) is dried in large kilns and is preferred to greenwood because it is less likely to warp or twist and less likely to split, especially at the end of boards.

Any wood contains natural defects: knots, splits and shakes, and cross grain. Because most of our work involves detailing and is readily seen (unlike framing which is usually covered), it is important that the wood we select be as perfect as possible, free of knots and split boards. It is a good idea to select wood yourself, rather than to order by phone, so that you get exactly the type you want.

Types of Wood

Some woods are hard, but others are soft and easily nailed into. Some woods cut more easily than others; some wood has a brownish tint; and so on. Let us consider the more popular building woods.

Douglas fir is a general building wood that is easy to work with, but it does not take finishings as well as others. Its color ranges from white to yellow, with a prominent grain.

Ash is used in baseball bats, which should give you some idea of its hardness. Ash is easy to work with and good for many household items. Its color ranges from gray to cream to red with a very straight grain.

Beech is a heavy, resilient wood that takes almost any finish and looks handsome. Its color is white to reddish with conspicuous rays on the surface.

Birch is a good, heavy wood with excellent shock resistance. It takes finishes well and is often used in cabinetmaking, but it is difficult to work on with hand tools. Its color is cream or light reddish brown.

Maple, a very handsome wood, generally used for flooring and furniture, is extremely hard and difficult to work with. Its color can be a modern-looking cream or the more traditional light reddish brown, with a prominent grain.

Pine is a relatively soft wood, easy to nail into and work with. It has a good resistance to shock and has dozens of uses, from construction to veneer. Pine is cream to light reddish brown in color.

Redwood has a prominent veining system. It is a soft wood that does not take shock well but is easy to work with. It resists decay and termites and takes finishes well, although it is quite handsome in its natural deep reddish brown.

Cedar is also used for interior work as well as porches where humidity may be a problem.

Oak has a prominent grain and needs filling to get a smooth surface. It is a hard, strong wood usually used for trim, and only sometimes for furniture. It is grayish yellow-brown with large rays.

PLYWOOD

Plywood is made from several layers of veneer (thin layers of wood) laid perpendicular to each other and bonded together with synthetic resin glues. The thickness of the plies varies, depending on what the wood is to be used for. Plywood is stronger, because of its thickness, than solid wood.

Cheap plywoods have core veneers of inferior quality; the joints between edges may not be perfectly mated; there may be knots or patches in them. You should select plywood in person rather than ordering by phone. Use marine grade or exterior-type plywood because they do not have gaps and are usually free of blemishes and knots. Plywood comes with both surfaces sanded or unsanded; unsanded plywood is not satisfactory for most uses. Sheets of plywood are available in several sizes—the smallest, 4 × 8 feet.

Where to Buy Lumber

Buying lumber can be confusing because it is available at lumberyards, at large home improvement stores, and at the bigger hardware and home supply centers. The difference is price, but sometimes the cheapest place to buy is not the best place.

LUMBERYARDS

If you feel lost in a lumberyard, you are not alone; most homeowners scouting for a few boards seem to be in the minority compared to the professional carpenters. However, invariably the old-fashioned lumber house will give you personal attention, answer dozens of questions, and take care of your needs. Lumberyards charge slightly higher prices, but often it is worth paying more because the quality of lumber is generally better. Lumber is the yards' bread-and-butter, so they stock the best.

HOME IMPROVEMENT STORES

Home improvement stores are springing up all over, and what they offer is convenience: that is, you can buy almost any type of hardware there, along with your lumber. These outlets cater almost exclusively to the noncarpenters, the homeowners who are doing it themselves.

In such a store the personalized touch is usually missing and you are very much on your own. Usually you will not see the lumber until it is delivered to your car. But if you know something about wood, you probably can get along fine here; if not, look elsewhere.

HOME SUPPLY CENTERS

These outlets fall somewhere between the lumberyards and the home improvement centers. Here you find cut-rate lumber along with dozens of household supplies, from sinks to bathroom vanities. It is a conglomerate that offers one-stop-convenience. However, I have found (and this is no condemnation) that usually the lumber (offered at lower prices than at lumberyards) is of lower quality. Shop in these outlets if you like, but be prepared to select your own wood and tote it home. Usually the help is not too erudite about lumber; you cannot expect them to be since they are selling more than 100 different products.

Salvage Materials

Should you buy salvage lumber? Most certainly—and doors and windows too if you can find them. They are inexpensive and some of the old doors and windows beat the new ones by miles. Used lumber is satisfactory too although it is climbing in price. You will find salvage items, especially doors and windows, at wrecking-house yards. Sales are often held at specific times of the year to give you even greater savings. True, it is a hassle to cart your own materials back home but you do save bucks. Look for pieces with character and those that can be used for a specific project. Don't be alarmed at the paint finish on some windows and doors; sandblasting the paint off is not that difficult or you can have it done professionally and it still is not costly.

You will find barn lumber and other used lumber offered in classified sections of your newspaper. Be wary with these purchases or you can end up with a bunch of lumber you do not have any use for. Shop carefully and inspect all materials first to see just what condition they are in. Lumber, unlike doors and windows where glass can be replaced and paint blasted off, must be in good structural condition. Inspect for cracks and splits and general appearance before you buy.

Flea markets and garage sales are other places you will find used materials. Here again it is a question of looking and using your imagination. I have one friend who bought sixteen shower doors and ended up making a distinctive greenhouse that is both functional and beautiful.

While you are shopping, look also for used hardware—door knobs, latches and such—because some of the old hardware is beautiful indeed and only needs cleaning. These fine pieces add a nice note of craftsmanship to a home and are usually far below the cost of new hardware.

Lumber Facts

Lumber can be sawed, drilled, and nailed with little trouble. But how to select the right grade of lumber? (There are many grades, just as there are grades in meats or clothing.) And how do you buy lumber? For example, when you buy a 2-×-4-foot piece of lumber, you do not really get a 2 × 4; the actual dimensions are 1 9/16 × 3 9/16.

Generally, your lumber dealer will advise you as to what you need, but I always believe in knowing something about what I am buying, not only to get my money's worth, but to work better with the material I am using. So here is information about how lumber is graded and sized.

Kiln-dried lumber is air-seasoned lumber without defects. *Greenwood lumber* has too much moisture and will shrink and pull loose from fastenings after a while.

The various grades of lumber have many surface textures. *Clear heartwood*, *A-grade*, and *common grade* are surfaced on both sides to a smooth finish. *Select heart* or *construction heart* may come from the mill with a rough surface. Saw-textured lumber is not the same as rough lumber; it is more expensive and has a handsome resawed quality.

Even within the specific grades of lumber there are variations, so it is a good idea, as mentioned, to personally select your lumber rather than having it selected for you. Also, frequently I have found that lumber is warped or not square. This is allowable in the lumber trade, but it can wreak havoc for the amateur carpenter. Again, select lumber in person.

Since the *actual* size of a piece of wood is not what the dimensions say, for easy reference here are tables of standard dimensions:

KILN-DRIED LUMBER

Size to Order	Actual Size
1 × 4	3/4 × 3 1/2
1 × 6	3/4 × 5 1/2
1 × 8	3/4 × 7 1/4
2 × 4	1 1/2 × 3 1/2
2 × 6	1 1/2 × 5 1/2
2 × 8	1 1/2 × 7 1/4

GREENWOOD LUMBER

Size to Order	Actual Size
1 × 3	25/32 × 2 9/16
1 × 4	25/32 × 3 9/16
1 × 6	25/32 × 5 5/8
1 × 8	25/32 × 7 1/4
2 × 3	1 9/16 × 2 9/16
2 × 4	1 9/16 × 3 9/16
2 × 6	1 9/16 × 5 5/8
2 × 8	1 9/16 × 7 1/2
2 × 10	1 9/16 × 9 1/2

Wood basics | 2

Most people know how to use a hammer or screwdriver when working with wood; still, a short review will help you immensely. (Note that some of the tools we mention are explained more fully in the next chapter.)

Nails

There are so many types of nails that it is important to use the right ones for the right jobs or you will waste a great deal of time. Nails are purchased by bulk weight or in boxes or plastic packages. Most nails are available in sizes from 2 to 20 penny. At one time the penny meant the price of 100 hand-forged nails; now the term means a nail's length.

The common or box nails are generally used for most construction. The box nail is thinner than the common nail and less likely to splinter wood. There are also scaffold nails, casing nails, coated sinkers, and finishing nails. They all more or less resemble each other except for the shape of their heads. They come in bright and galvanized finish. The casing or finishing nail is used for detail work like moldings.

If you want rustproof nails, use galvanized stainless steel, copper, or aluminum nails. It is safe to use a nail that measures three times as long as the thickness of the board you are using. Nails with sharp points are preferred over the blunt-nosed nail, and thinner nails should be used for hardwood rather than for softwood.

NAILING

To brush up on your nailing techniques, use a scrap piece of lumber. With soft woods you can nail without making a pilot hole, but if you are going to be using hardwoods, you have to make a pilot hole with a nail punch or another nail. The pilot hole should be slightly smaller than the diameter of the nail and about two-thirds of its length. Hold the hammer near the end of its handle, and start the nail with light taps while holding it in place with your fingers. Once the nail is started, remove your fingers and take full swings, using the wrist and arm. If a nail bends slightly, change the striking angle to get the nail straight into the wood. However, if the nail bends severely, remove it and start with a new one. As the nail gets level with the surface of the wood, ease up on the power.

Nails driven at a slant hold better than nails driven straight down into wood. For an item with several parts, say, an intricate window, first clamp the wood pieces together and then nail. The clamp or vise lets you use both hands, one for holding the item, one for nailing.

Toenailing is driving a nail into wood at an angle, generally in corners or where nails cannot be driven from the outside surface. Toenailing takes a little practice, so do not get discouraged if your first attempts fail.

If you have to insert nails at the end of a board, do it carefully or the wood will split. And driving nails in closely together in a line can also split wood, so stagger the nail holes. Always nail against rather than into the grain. If joining two boards, be sure the nail is long enough to join them, but not so long that it goes through the boards. The length of the nail should be 1/4 inch less than the total depth of the two boards.

Whenever possible drive nails on the inside of pieces of wood rather than on the outside so they will not show. Nail heads showing are no disaster but if they can be avoided, so much the better.

Hammering Know-how

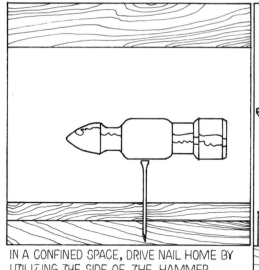

IN A CONFINED SPACE, DRIVE NAIL HOME BY UTILIZING THE SIDE OF THE HAMMER.

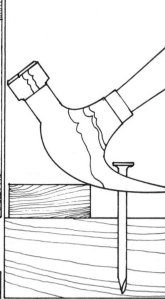

BLOCK OF WOOD UNDER HAMMER MAKES EXTRACTING NAIL EASIER.

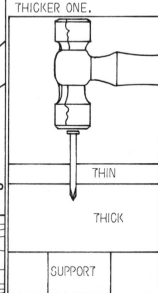

ALWAYS NAIL THINNER WOOD TO THICKER ONE.

THIN

THICK

SUPPORT

ADEQUATE SUPPORT AVOIDS BENDING OR SKIDDING.

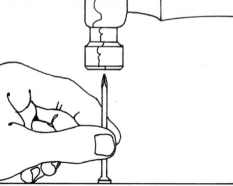

AVOID SPLITTING WOOD BY BLUNTING NAILING POINTS.

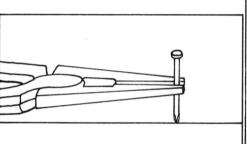

HOLD SMALL NAIL WITH LONG-NOSED PLIERS FOR EASIER HAMMERING.

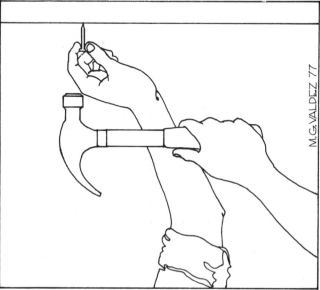

M.G. VALDEZ 77

LEANING BACKWARDS FOR NAILING OVERHEAD CAN BE MADE EASY BY USING THE NORMAL FORWARD HAMMER STROKE.

To remove a nail, lift it out with the claw end of the hammer (not as easy as you think). There is a small ledge at the bottom of the V between the claws; you must get this edge under the head of the nail. When the claw is engaged, roll the hammer on the curve of the head. Move the claw into a vertical position to lift the nail; let the claw loose and move it at an angle and insert a block of wood under the hammer head. Now apply leverage on the handle and remove the nail with a fast jerk. Some nails, such as finishing (casing) nails, defy removal because they do not have heads.

Screws

Like nails, wood screws come in various sizes and with different heads. You can buy screws from 1/4 inch in length to 3 inches. Screws have flat heads or rounded heads, and slots may be flat, oval, or round. There is also a Phillip's-head screw, which has a cross slot. The diameters of screws vary from 1/8 inch to 1/2 inch. Screws are available in several finishes. Use fine-headed screws (threads close together) for hardwood; use coarser threaded screws for softwood. Choose a screw for woodwork so that at least one-half of its threaded length will enter the base of the wood.

INSTALLING SCREWS

Always use screws that are the proper length and width for the thickness of your wood. It is very difficult to install a screw without a pilot hole; in fact, it is damn hard, so by all means use a predrilled starting hole, or make the hole with an awl. The pilot hole should be slightly smaller than the diameter of the screw used. For the screw to hold in the wood, the entire length of the threaded part of the screw should penetrate the base piece of wood.

Flat-head and oval-head screws should be countersunk so they are flush with the wood. To do this, drill a beveled hole equal to the diameter of the screwhead. Drill this hole after you do the pilot hole for the screw; thus, you have to drill two holes for countersunk screws.

Driving a screw into wood is a simple operation if you have matched the screwdriver to the shape, width, and length of the slot of the screw. Otherwise it can be a mess. Use the screwdriver with a firm grip and a steady turning motion, neither too hard nor too soft. If the screw seems too hard to drive into the wood, use a little soap on the threads to lubricate them. Try to keep screwdrivers sharp and properly shaped. (You can file heads to make them smooth.)

Glues

Today there are excellent wood epoxies and glues that make joining boards and attaching wood members quite easy. Some are miraculously strong and could *probably* be used by themselves without any other fasteners, but it is wise to drive a few nails in place.

Select a heavy-duty glue recommended by hardware store personnel. If you are going to do extensive gluing, it will be necessary to hold the pieces of wood together while the glue sets. Clamps are sold at hardware stores, or hold the pieces in a vise until they set.

When you apply the glue, try to put it exactly where the joints come together; do not get it all over the wood. Be on target, and use just enough so that when the pieces of wood are pressed together only a slight residue escapes at the edges. Immediately wipe off excess glue with a cloth.

Sawing

To start a saw cut, brace the saw against the thumb; now draw the saw back and make several short cuts. The simple first cut will make sawing easy because the saw then has a guideline cut to get it moving. Now, holding the saw at a 60-degree angle, saw with long easy strokes, neither too fast nor too slow. Once the saw is moving, keep up the stroking and cutting. If the saw leaves the line, turn the handle slightly so the blade can get back to the guideline.

How to Measure and Saw Wood

THE CORRECT WAY TO MARK WITH SQUARE IS BY HOLDING PENCIL TILTED SLIGHTLY.

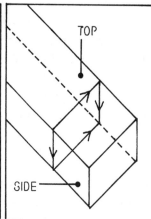

FOR PERFECT SQUARE CUT, RUN TOP, BOTTOM AND SIDE LINES IN SAME DIRECTION.

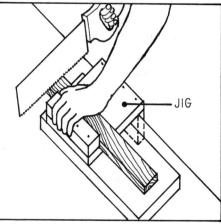

A BENCH HOOK JIG HELPS TO STEADY SMALL WOOD.

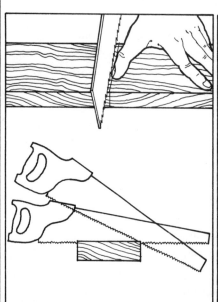

TO START CUT, STEADY SAW WITH THUMBNAIL AND DRAW BACK SEVERAL TIMES UNTIL BLADE "LOCKS" INTO CUTTING PATTERN. CUT AT 45° ANGLE.

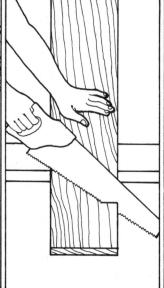

DURING CUT, STEADY LUMBER WITH ONE HAND. BEFORE CUT IS COMPLETED, HOLD CUT-OFF PIECE TO AVOID SPLINTERING.

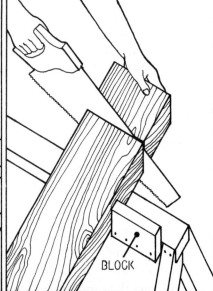

CUTTING HEAVY LUMBER REQUIRES THE SAFETY OF BLOCK SUPPORT OR C-CLAMP AGAINST HAZARDOUS MOVEMENT.

To guide a saw for an accurate cut, use a block of wood with a squared end flush to the side of the blade. When using a crosscut saw, hold the saw at a 45-degree angle to the wood. When you get close to the end of the wood, support the cut-off piece to prevent splintering. Use the coping saw for curved cuts; hold the wood in a vise vertically and point the teeth of the saw away from you so the cut is made with the push stroke. Use horizontal strokes with the backsaw.

If you are cutting a thin slice from the end of a board, place the board on a piece of scrap. Start the cut in the scrap board and follow through. If possible, clamp the two boards together.

Making Wood Joints

Probably the most important aspect of wood construction is joining ends, and there are a variety of ways to do it. The most common and easiest joint for the beginner is the butt joint, which is put together straight or right angled and is nailed or screwed in place, one piece of lumber to the other. Sometimes glue is used in addition to the nails or screws. The butt joint eliminates the angled or mitered cut, but for aesthetics—where you want a neat appearance—the mitered cut is best. In the miter cut no end grain is visible. The miter is cut with a miter box, at a 45-degree angle. The miter joint is not as strong as the butt joint.

The lap joint, frequently used, is easy to do. The lap joint is an L shape; you cut away a section of one board and a section of the joining board and then put them together like a sandwich. This joint is usually glued and nailed. There are several variations of the lap joint, such as cross lap and middle lap joints, but the principle is the same: a recess is cut in one side to hide most of the grain, and the board is set flush in place and glued and nailed.

A mortise and tenon joint is exceptionally strong; this is a T shape. The mortise is the slot on the left piece of wood, and the tenon is the tongue on the right. This is fitted into the mortise with glue.

There are other types of joints, but basically these are the ones you will work with. See Page 16 for a variety of joints.

Joints

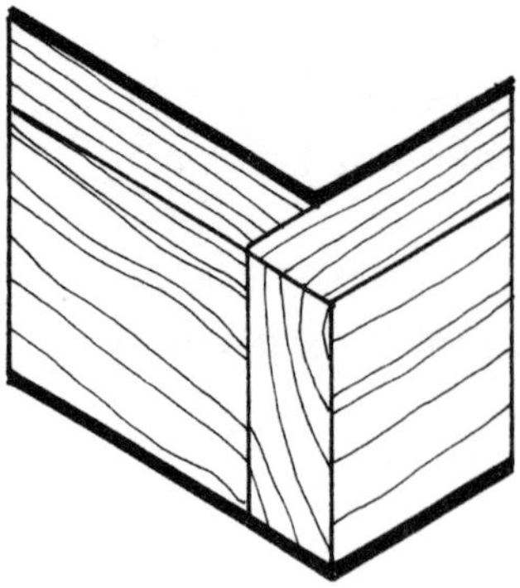

BUTT JOINT

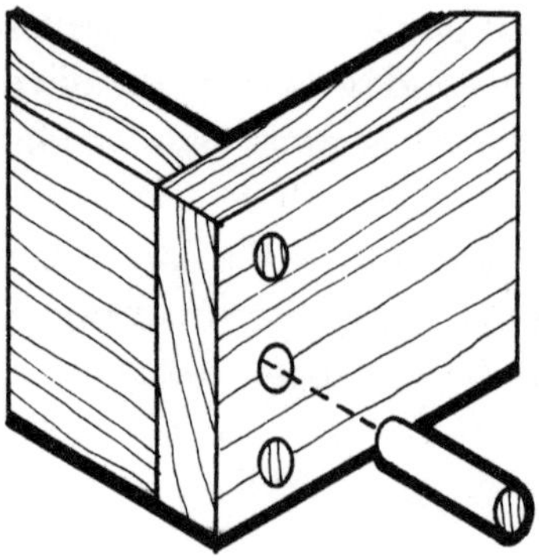

DOWEL JOINT

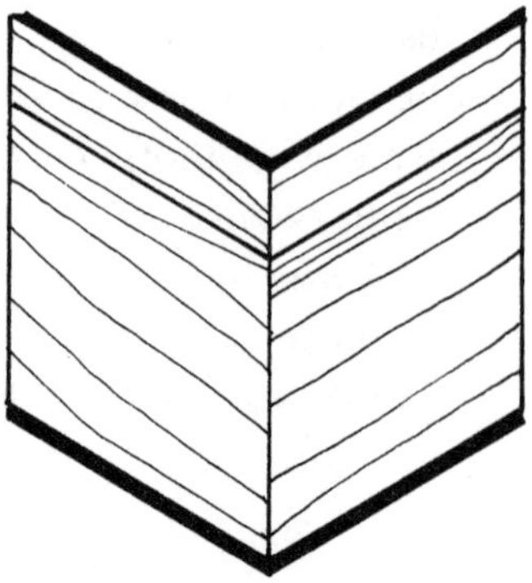

MITERED JOINT

LAP

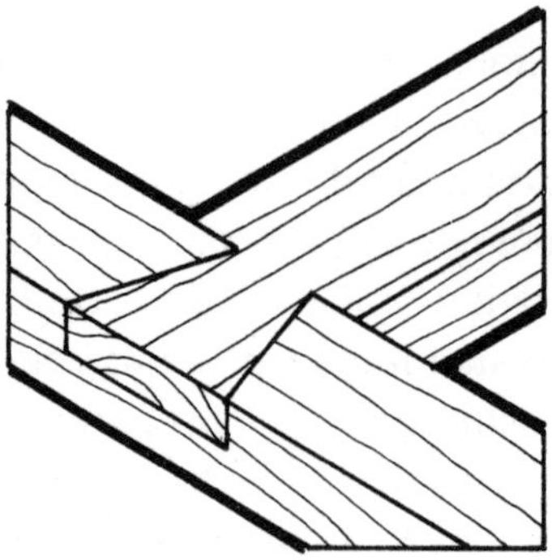

DOVETAIL

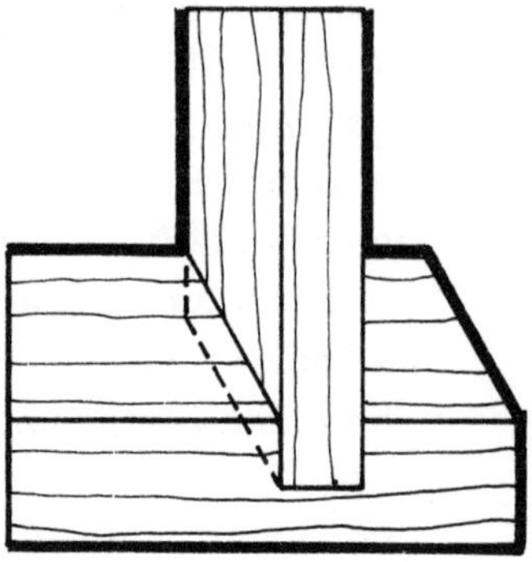

DADO

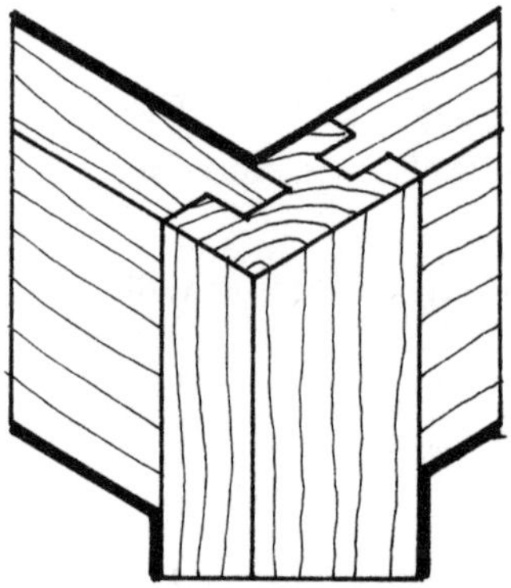

TONGUE AND GROOVE

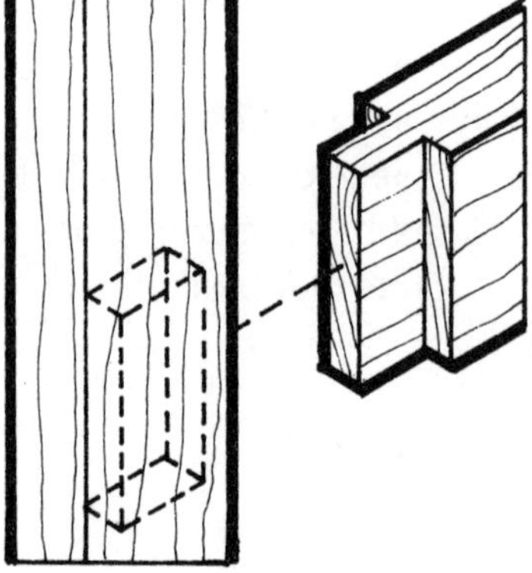

MORTISE AND TENON

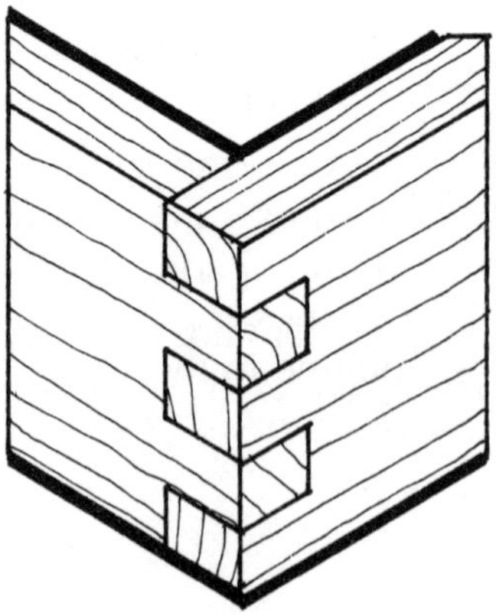

BOX JOINTS

Wood Terms

Perhaps better called "construction terms," these are various words used to describe the pieces in standard construction. For each part of house construction—doors and windows, floors, ceilings, walls—there are terms for describing the wood members; a working knowledge of these terms will help you in ordering lumber and in doing construction. When we talk of walls we talk about studs and top plates and sole plates. Window and door construction includes words like trimmer stud and header, sill and so forth. Ceiling work includes beams and rafters, joists, and in floor work there are joists and subflooring. Drawings D & E will show you some of these parts of building.

Permits and Building Codes

Building codes vary from state to state; these are codes adopted by the city or township to assure that houses are built properly and to maximum safety standards. Even if you are remodeling (and not building a house from the ground up) it is wise to check building codes to determine which materials are allowed (for fire safety, etc.) and which are not. Check your phone book for the Building Code Office, generally in the city hall or city center. The office will advise you if a permit is necessary to build a certain component. If you are doing minor remodeling—replacing a window, for instance—usually no permit is necessary. Still, it is wise to check first, not later. The cost of a building permit is usually nominal.

Professional Help

You can, of course, enlist professional help for some of the jobs we outline in this book. Although we give instructions for pouring a concrete floor, many times it is wiser to have this part of remodeling done by a

Construction Parts

A

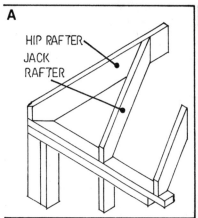

HIP RAFTER
JACK RAFTER

B

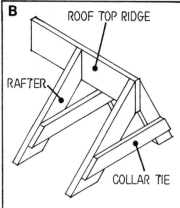

ROOF TOP RIDGE
RAFTER
COLLAR TIE

C

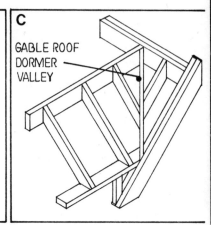

GABLE ROOF DORMER VALLEY

D

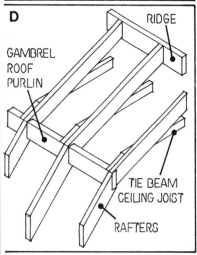

RIDGE
GAMBREL ROOF PURLIN
TIE BEAM CEILING JOIST
RAFTERS

E

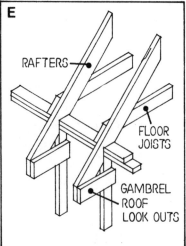

RAFTERS
FLOOR JOISTS
GAMBREL ROOF LOOK OUTS

F

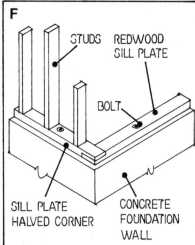

STUDS   REDWOOD SILL PLATE
BOLT
SILL PLATE HALVED CORNER
CONCRETE FOUNDATION WALL

G

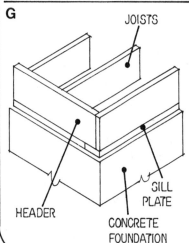

JOISTS
HEADER
SILL PLATE
CONCRETE FOUNDATION

A HIP AND JACK RAFTERS

B ROOF TOP RIDGE AND COLLAR TIE

C ROOF VALLEY ON GABLE ROOF

D PURLIN ON GAMBREL ROOF SECURED BY TIE BEAM JOIST

E LOOK OUTS ON GAMBREL ROOF

F SILL PLATE HALVED CORNER

G HEADER AND JOIST ON SILL PLATE

Construction Parts

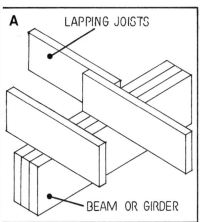

A LAPPING JOISTS / BEAM OR GIRDER

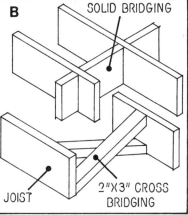

B SOLID BRIDGING / JOIST / 2"X3" CROSS BRIDGING

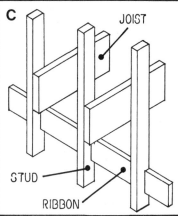

C JOIST / STUD / RIBBON

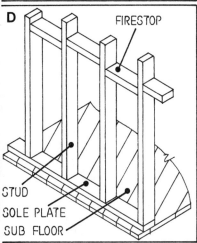

D FIRESTOP / STUD / SOLE PLATE / SUB FLOOR

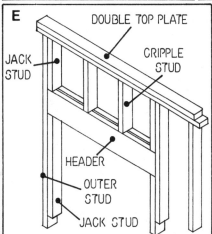

E DOUBLE TOP PLATE / CRIPPLE STUD / JACK STUD / HEADER / OUTER STUD / JACK STUD

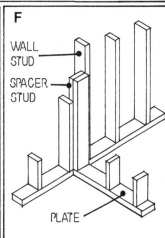

F WALL STUD / SPACER STUD / PLATE

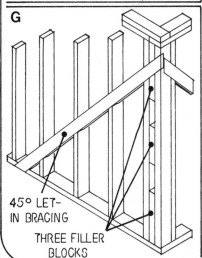

G 45° LET-IN BRACING / THREE FILLER BLOCKS

A FLOOR JOISTS ON WOOD BEAM OR GIRDER

B FLOOR JOISTS SECURED BY BRIDGING

C RIBBON BEARING JOISTS

D FIRESTOP (FIREBLOCKING) BETWEEN STUDS

E WINDOW OR DOOR HEADER WITH CRIPPLE AND JACK STUDS

F SPACER STUD FOR PARTITION WALL

G DIAGONAL LET-IN (KNOTCHED INTO STUDS AND CORNER) BRACES AND THREE FILLER BLOCKS IN CORNER POST CONSTRUCTION

professional. It takes a lot less time. On the other hand, it all depends on your own expertise and ability to follow directions. Roofing is another area that is perhaps better left to a professional although if you are doing patch work on relatively small areas you may want to try it.

Wood Tools | 3

Saws

The saw is the universal cutting tool; you can use reliable handsaws or the more convenient and faster power saws. The handsaws used in small carpentry work are the crosscut saw, backsaw, compass saw, and coping saw. The power saws are the saber saw, band saw, circular saw, and continuous band saw. Saw length varies from 12 to 26 inches. A coarse tooth is better on thicker and softer woods; a fine tooth gives a cleaner edge. Also, a narrow blade cuts tighter curves than a wide blade.

HANDSAWS

The standard crosscut saw is the handsaw you will use the most. It is used for cutting across the grain and is narrower at the tip than at the handle.

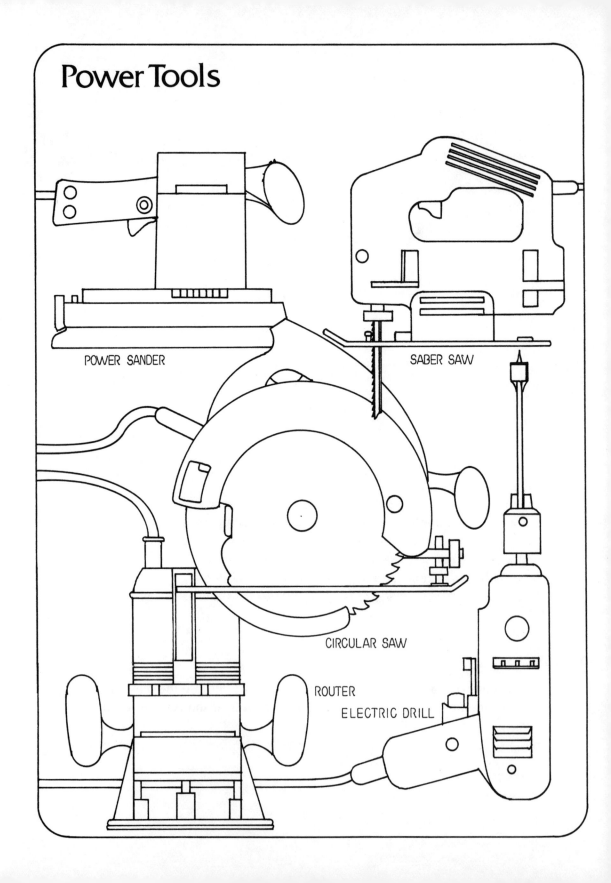

Power Tools

POWER SANDER

SABER SAW

CIRCULAR SAW

ROUTER

ELECTRIC DRILL

The compass saw has a V-shaped blade about 12 to 16 inches long secured in a small rectangular frame. It is used for accurate cuts and curves. Another type of compass saw, the coping saw, makes fine curve cutting easy. The end of the blade is held by a loop or pin. A backsaw looks like a handsaw but has the same width blade at the handle and end. It is used for cutting joints and for general bench work.

PORTABLE POWER SAWS

A power saw may cut with a circular blade, a continuous band, or a short stiff blade, as in a saber saw. The circular saw is for straight cuts; the continuous band and saber saws are for cutting curves, with the saber saw being preferred because it is not restricted by the size of the area between the blade and the support. A saber saw is highly recommended because it is basically a portable jigsaw; since the end of the blade is free, it can cut both enclosed and external curves. The saber saw blade is stiff but not long and works on an up-and-down motion. The band saw, used for cutting both irregular and straight shapes, comes with a choice of blades. (Various types of power saws are also available as table models.)

The depth of a cut is adjusted by the small table the saw projects through; this enables you to see ahead the line you are cutting. The standard electric portable power saw is 8 to 10 inches in diameter powered by a 1-horsepower motor.

TABLE POWER SAWS

The basic table or bench saw is the circular saw, which is used for straight-line cutting, crosscutting, and ripping long boards. By tilting the blade you can achieve bevel cuts of any angle up to 45 degrees. The saw has a sturdy table and an arbor, (a protective hood) and motor; the blade is

Hand Tools

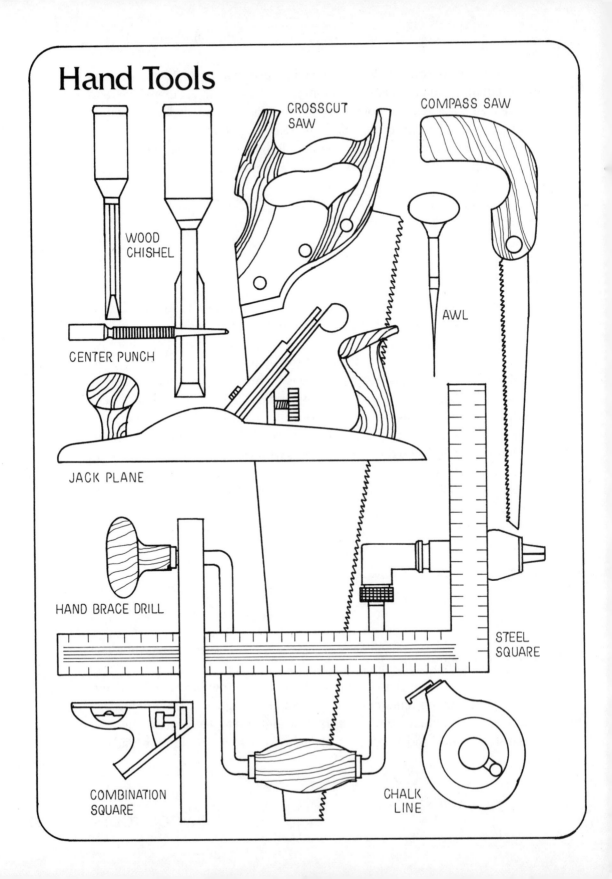

WOOD
CHISHEL

CROSSCUT
SAW

COMPASS SAW

CENTER PUNCH

AWL

JACK PLANE

HAND BRACE DRILL

STEEL
SQUARE

COMBINATION
SQUARE

CHALK
LINE

secured to the arbor and driven by a motor with belts and pulleys. There are numerous circular saw blades, from crosscut to ripsaw.

The radial arm saw does basically everything the circular saw does and has the extra advantage of being easy to use because it cuts from above the work. Layout marks are always in view on top of the wood. The saw remains stationary while the saw blade is moved over the work. The saw has a yoke-mounted motor suspended from a horizontal arm—the arm is mounted on a sturdy column at the rear. The motor, yoke, and horizontal arm can be adjusted to any desired angle. With various accessories the radial arm saw can grind, sand, shape, and rout.

The band saw makes bevel cuts up to 45 degrees. With this saw you can easily do compound cutting and pattern sawing. The blade is of flexible steel, with the ends welded together to form a continuous band. The blade is set over two large wheels, the size of the band saw is measured by the wheel diameter.

The jigsaw is actually a motor-driven coping saw and, like the band and saber saws, makes irregular cuts. Its advantage is that it can do fine precision work. The machine has a very fine thin blade held between two chucks, one below and one above the worktable.

Power Drills

The portable electric drill is as essential to remodeling as the hammer and screwdriver. You can use an old-fashioned hand drill, but the power drill is easier to use and far superior. If you have a small hand drill (these are the egg beater-type drills that use up to 1/4-inch diameter bits), by all means use it.

The most common electric drill has a 1/4-inch diameter; the diameter refers to the size of the neck that clamps around the bit. You want a drill with a geared-key, Jacobs-type chuck to center and grip the bit. These trigger-type drills operate on standard household current but require three-hole grounded sockets to prevent shock. With a power hand drill you essentially have many tools in one because you can use a variety of

Hammers and Screwdrivers

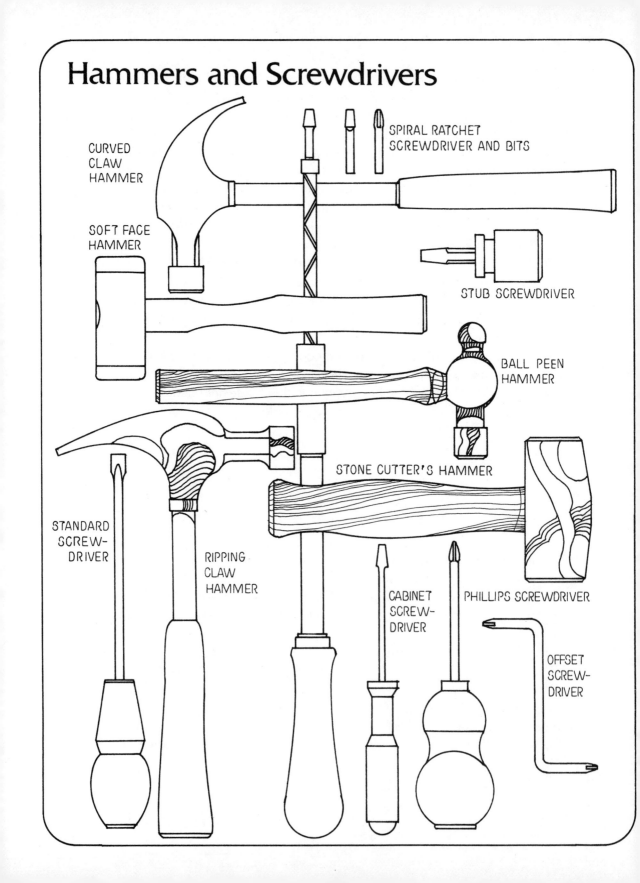

CURVED
CLAW
HAMMER

SPIRAL RATCHET
SCREWDRIVER AND BITS

SOFT FACE
HAMMER

STUB SCREWDRIVER

BALL PEEN
HAMMER

STONE CUTTER'S HAMMER

STANDARD
SCREW-
DRIVER

RIPPING
CLAW
HAMMER

CABINET
SCREW-
DRIVER

PHILLIPS SCREWDRIVER

OFFSET
SCREW-
DRIVER

attachments to make the drill a sander or a saber saw, for example. Check local hardware stores for drill attachments.

You can buy almost sixty different bits for your electric drill, but generally all you will need is a kit of seven or eight. Treat your drill with kindness; it is the only way to make it last a long time.

Use an easy pressure, letting the bit do the work. Try not to overheat the drill by using excessive pressure and speed. Keep bits sharp, and do not use bits wider than the diameter of the chuck. To drill holes, mark the diameter of the hole and its exact position on the wood with a pencil; keep in mind the depth you want to drill into the wood: halfway, one-quarter way through, and so forth (or clean through). Center the drill firmly in the center of the circle. Hold it perpendicular to the wood and start the drilling process. Work on a waist-high, level table. Drill easily but steadily until the desired depth is reached.

Follow the safety rules that come with a drill, and wear goggles when drilling to protect your eyes from flying debris.

Hammers

There are dozens of hammers available, from an upholsterer's hammer to the standard household hammer. The two basic types are the adze-eye hammer and the claw hammer; each has a wooden handle or a steel shaft. There are two types of claw hammers: the curved and the ripping. The curved claw is preferred because it provides more leverage when you are pulling nails. Hammer faces (the surfaces that actually hit the nails) can be convex or flat; the flat face lets you drive in a nail without marring wood surfaces.

A patternmaker's hammer is also an invaluable tool to have on hand for making small items. A 6-ounce one is just about right. A small upholsterer's hammer is helpful because it has a narrow head, weighs little, and can get into places that the standard claw hammer cannot reach. Hammers come in long and short lengths. The long ones give you more leverage, and the short ones are ideal for more ordinary work. Hammer weights also vary. A 14- to 16-ounce hammerhead is fine for most work and suits most people. Use a hammer that feels good in your hand.

You may be tempted to use a squeeze-type stapler for lightweight fastening jobs, but generally these do not ensure the solid bonds necessary in woodwork.

Screwdrivers

There are dozens of sizes and kinds of screwdrivers available. Buy four or five with different sized heads—an ill-fitting screwdriver can lead to trouble as well as frustration. The blade of the screwdriver should fit snugly into the screw slot. If the screwdriver fits too loosely, it is almost impossible to drive in the screw properly. Buy the large standard-type screwdriver with a square shank, and remember that a long screwdriver gives you more power than a short-handled one and is less likely to tilt in the screw slot. It is best to have one long-handled screwdriver, an intermediate size, and a couple of jewelers' screwdrivers. Jewelers' screwdrivers are small, with short handles, and great for getting into tight places.

A magnetized screwdriver will help keep you from losing screws. It is perfect if you are doing extensive carpentry and know how to handle it, though it does take some getting used to. Ratchet-type screwdrivers (operated by the motion of the handle) are extremely handy once you get the hang of them.

Marking Tools

Quite frankly, the best tools for marking cuts on wood are a good heavy lead pencil and a ruler—you will use both these tools repeatedly. A grease pencil can also be used, but it leaves a wider line, which can distort dimensions unless you take into account the width of the line.

The combination square can be used as a level, marking gage, or depth gage. The handle slides along a channel in the blade; by a small knob you adjust the distance the handle moves. A chalk line is a long spool-wound cord fitted into a container filled with chalk. The string is pulled from the container, stretched across a piece of wood, and snapped downward, leaving a clear chalk-mark line.

A marking gage marks lines parallel to a board. The gage has a thick rounded rule that can be tightened down at any specific mark. A mark is scratched with a sharp pin at the edge of the rule as the block rides along the board edge.

A very important tool is a wing divider. This tool lays out round lines, such as rounded corners. It is also useful for making circles and arcs. A wing divider looks like the old school compass; the difference is that there are two metal-edged points, and the distance between the points is adjusted by a screw device.

Planes

You will need a plane to remove unwanted portions of wood from a board or molding. As opposed to a chisel, you can control the depth and width of the cut with a plane. The bench and block plane are used for general carpentry.

The block plane is small, can be manipulated with one hand, and is used for smoothing with the grain along a board's length. Bench planes come in three sizes: the jointer plane, the jack plane, and the smooth plane. A long plane is best because it smooths wood easily; short ones have a tendency to ride up and down. The jack plane is the best for our work and measures from 12 to 15 inches; it is excellent for removing irregularities on wood. The small bench plane is about 6 inches long and is used for smoothing surfaces after the jack plane has been used.

It is important to know exactly how to use a plane or you will ruin the wood with it. Sight down the plane's underside, and be sure the blade edge is protruding only slightly through the opening and is perfectly square across. If it is not, adjust it with the screw cap until it is. Angle the bench plane to get a shearing cut, and always cut in the same direction as the grain of the wood. Keep the cuts shallow but always even. Use more pressure at the front knob, and plane in short even strokes.

The blade on a plane should be cutting sharp at all times, so have a whetting stone on hand.

Holding Tools

You need various clamping tools to hold pieces of wood together while you saw, drill, nail, or glue them. Whenever you use clamping tools, protect the wood surfaces you are working on by fitting a scrap of lumber between the jaws and wood block.

The woodworker's vise is perhaps the most useful of the holding tools; this versatile tool clamps onto a workbench or table and holds many materials securely so you can work on them. Buy a vise with large jaws, and when bench- or table-mounting a vise, keep the top of the jaws flush with the table top.

The C clamp, another useful holding device, has jaws from 3 to 16 inches in width. The C clamp can be attached to a workbench. Spring clamps look like large clothespins and are fine for clamping light work. They have two spring-loaded handles that keep the jaws clamped tight until the handles are squeezed together.

There are other holding and clamping tools, but usually the vise and C clamp are all that are needed for woodwork.

Other Equipment

In addition to the standard tools, you will need a sawhorse which you can build from 2 × 4s or buy a commercial one. Here is a case where I suggest you buy one instead of making it yourself. It is essential to have a good sturdy sawhorse to hold wood while you cut. I still use my old homemade one but the new sawhorses I see at stores are more durable; I will no doubt succumb to purchasing one soon.

You will need ladders—generally one 12-foot ladder and an extension 18-to-24-foot type. If you have to have scaffolding, then of course you will need two ladders the same size. (You can rent both scaffolding and ladders.)

Tarpaulin cloths to cover and protect finished areas of construction come in handy; tarps, as they are called, are expensive so you might want to use the inexpensive plastic sheeting sold at paint stores. Or raid the family rag-bag for old bedspreads or sheets. If you are putting in a skylight you won't want to mar the finished floor; the tarp protects it. Use it.

A wheelbarrow comes in handy for dozens of jobs when you are remodeling. You, of course, transport things in it and it can also be used for mixing mortar. By all means get the best wheelbarrow you can afford; the cheap ones invariably fall apart in a few short months.

Helpful Hints

Tools are one thing, but a good friend to help you when you are remodeling is another. If possible, have a friend give you a hand. Many of the construction jobs, such as handling a 4-×-8-foot piece of plywood, really require four hands. Handling long rafters and beams if you are redoing a ceiling also requires the help of another person. And if you are working on a ceiling you will realize that two people can do the job in half the time. It saves one person running down and up the ladder to get lumber. Your spouse or sturdy teen-ager qualify as friends when it comes to remodeling.

One last thing: although we do not anticipate accidents when you work with wood and tools, there are likely to be cuts and bruises. Keep a good first-aid kit on hand. Nobody is perfect.

Welcome: Arbors and Archways | 4

Too often, when people start to rebuild or remodel at home they forget a very important aspect of good total planning. Busy with the interior of the house, they neglect the approach to the house, yet this is where the guest first gets an impression of what is to come. The entrance, walkway, or approach to the house can and does reflect what is inside the home; it is vitally important to the overall plan. The beauty of arbors, loggias, or pergolas (besides their obvious attractiveness) is that they provide an old-world charm to an entrance. And adding small details like an arbor or an archway can be done easily in a weekend.

Arbors

The arbor, the craftsman's tour de force in old England, was the introduction to many a charming cottage. These structures have dimension and beauty and provide a restful, shady area, a place to pause before going inside. With an arbor, you do not need a gate, and the arbor serves as an additional small living area as it defines the property. It is also a guidepost that says: "Here is the welcoming entrance to our house."

Because it is so visually prominent, the arbor must be built with the utmost attention to detail, pattern, and proportion. True, you can crisscross sticks in any pattern and still come out with a reasonably charming effect, but the carefully executed arbor will be a stunning sight. With arbors you are working with specific designs, so preplanning on paper is definitely necessary.

What distance from the house should the arbor be placed? There is no hard and fast rule but if the length of the entrance longitudinally is 50 feet, the arbor placed midpoint (25 feet) will work well. It is not too close to the street or the house and is a pleasing feature.

The basic construction of arbors requires trelliswork, that is, laths or sticks nailed into a diamond or grid pattern. (See photos.) Laths are the thin wooden strips used in latticework and plasterwork; lath is usually redwood or cedar, about 3/8 inch thick and 1 5/8 inches wide. It is sold in bundles of 6, 8, and 10 feet (fifty pieces). Generally, two grades of laths are milled; one grade has some defects like knotholes and blemishes; the other grade is surfaced and smooth. The latter grade is best for arbors.

You can build a somewhat sturdier arbor from 2-×-2-inch wood strips cut to size. This construction is more expensive than that done with lathing, but it is stronger and better looking. Run strips lengthwise from front to back, spaced at 12- or 16-inch intervals, and set wooden rafters as shown in Drawing 1.

Another type of arbor is made from batten (as in the phrase "board and batten"). Battens are large laths 1/4 to 3/4 inch thick and 1 to 2 inches wide. Battens are sold in lengths up to 20 feet, by the piece or bundle, thirty pieces to the bundle. They cost about 20 percent more than laths. Battens are smooth-surfaced and have more strength than lathing. Battens are recommended for very decorative arbors.

As mentioned, most lathing is redwood or cedar, and these woods weather beautifully to a silver sheen or can be painted white. You can also use pine or fir, but these woods need a coating, such as paint or other wood-protective products.

Entrance Arbor

(1) CAST CONCRETE FOOTINGS IN PLACE WITH METAL POST CONNECTORS

(2) TEMPORARILY BRACE 4 x 4 POSTS IN POSITION & BOLT TO CONNECTORS

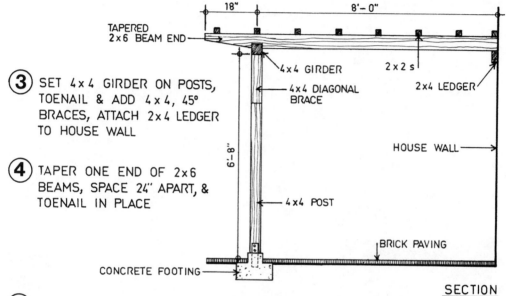

TAPERED
2 x 6 BEAM END

18"   8'- 0"

4 x 4 GIRDER

4 x 4 DIAGONAL
BRACE

2 x 2 s

2 x 4 LEDGER

(3) SET 4 x 4 GIRDER ON POSTS, TOENAIL & ADD 4 x 4, 45° BRACES, ATTACH 2 x 4 LEDGER TO HOUSE WALL

HOUSE WALL

(4) TAPER ONE END OF 2 x 6 BEAMS, SPACE 24" APART, & TOENAIL IN PLACE

6'- 8"

4 x 4 POST

BRICK PAVING

CONCRETE FOOTING

SECTION

(5) NAIL 2 x 2 CROSS PIECES 16" APART, ON TOP

NOTE: USE REDWOOD & GALVANIZED NAILS

2011954

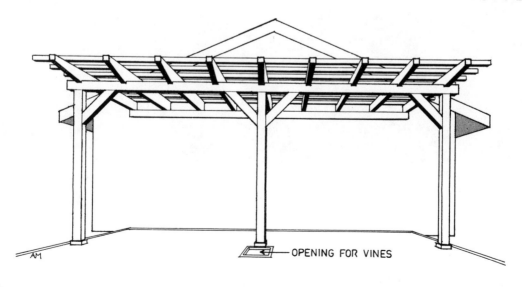

OPENING FOR VINES

AM

A pergola-type entrance adds charm and dimension to this small house; trellis is the basic construction.

Here a trellis archway is used to signal the entrance to a home; there is great character and an intimate feeling in the arch-type construction.

Close-up of the wooden construction of trelliswork.

FINISHING TOUCHES

CONSTRUCTION

Most arbors and lattices are constructed by epoxying and nailing a lath upon a lath in a cross-type pattern. There is also an interlocking type of construction, which is stronger than the other method and looks more finished than crisscross glued lattice. No instruction is needed for the standard type of lattice-building, but for the interlocking method follow these nine rules:

1. Use 1 × 1s or 2 × 2s.
2. Tape together bundles of wood (ten pieces to a bundle) with ends flush.
3. Mark all pieces with parallel 1-inch wide lines. Space lines evenly.
4. Tape masking tape lengthwise on your saw to a 1-inch depth for 2-inch strips. Saw down as far as the tape, just inside your markings.
5. With a small hammer strike between the saw cuts to knock out the chunk of wood; this leaves a socket or groove.
6. Insert 1-×-1-inch wood strips crosswise into the grooves (they should fit flush).
7. Use 4 × 4 posts as frames.
8. Nail strips into grooved pieces.
9. Paint the arbor, or leave it natural.

Correct spacing of laths in arbor work is vitally important if you want to create a definite pattern. For lathing 1/32 inch thick, use a 3/4-inch space. For lathing 2 × 2 inches, use a 1 1/2-inch space. No matter what space you use between laths, keep it constant throughout the pattern. For a spacer, use a wood block inserted between the laths as you nail them in place. A block 6 to 8 inches long works fine. Lay it flat on top to nail the lath in place and then again near the bottom to nail the bottom of the lath in place.

When you have figured the total area of the latticework and the size of the members and the spacing, you can determine how much lumber will be needed for the project. To determine how much wood you need, divide width of the lath plus the space between laths into 12 to get number of running feet of lath required per square foot:

For example, if you are using 1 1/2-inch lath spaced 1/2 inch apart,

$$\frac{12}{\text{Width} + \text{space}} = \text{Running feet/square foot}$$

$$\frac{12}{1.5 + 0.5} = \frac{12}{2} = 6$$

To determine the total number of running feet you need to cover an area, multiply the running feet per square foot by the total number of square feet in the area. For instance, if there are 6 running feet of lathing per square foot and 50 square feet to cover, order 300 running feet of lath—6 × 50 = 300.

If you are buying bundled lath, figure the number of running feet per bundle and divide this amount into the number of running feet needed. To find the number of running feet per bundle, multiply the length of the lath by the number of laths in a bundle. Thus, a bundle of 50 laths of 6-foot lengths is 300 running feet.

Substantial framing is necessary for the arbor; usually four 4 × 4 posts work well. (See Drawing 1.) Nail the frame together at corners and further brace the frame with diagonal braces on each post's corner. Set the posts into the ground at least 18 inches, and anchor them with concrete. Be sure the posts are in absolute alignment with each other before you start nailing lathing in place.

The arch is the most difficult part of the arbor to build, so if you are not too handy with carpentry, you might want to use a straight top, which is easy to make.

PATTERNS

The grid pattern is the easiest to make. Simply nail and epoxy the lathing top and bottom horizontally; then repeat the procedure, nailing the other laths vertically to each end of the horizontal laths. The spacing for the grid pattern is usually 1 inch.

The basket-weave pattern is handsome but somewhat difficult to build. The laths are alternated: each lath is pushed under and over another lath to create a woven effect.

The original house before construction was started; there is a plain unappealing look about it with no sense of entrance at all. There is room for vast improvement here.

The same house with original entrance removed and French windows added—the entrance is still unappealing and needs some dimension.

The diamond pattern is a variation of the grid and easy to make. Instead of nailing horizontally and vertically, nail diagonally.

Geometrical and starburst effects are also possible, but these patterns require *precise* laying out of the structure on the ground, nailing together, and attaching to frames.

Arbors can be left bare—they make a handsome decorative accent—or of course can be used for vining plants.

Archways/Pergolas

The trellis archway brings the beauty of the curve into focus at the entrance to the house. The archway is a tunnel placed strategically so it is focused on the doorway of the home. The archway adds perspective, relieves the bareness of many entrance grounds, and provides a unique effect, which is why it is now being used more than ever.

Archways require more construction than arbors, but the construction is easy because it usually consists simply of straight sides on a series of posts (see Drawing 2). The overhead can repeat the curve pattern or have the flat roof effect of trellises. To make the arch top, use benderboard—this is a redwood veneer material that can be bent to shape. (You can also use conventional wood and cut and shape to an arch, but it is more work.)

A pergola is a structure that frames a view or adds interest to a house entrance. Once a crude pole structure, the pergola can now be made into infinite designs by using crossed members of wood. A pergola is similar to an archway but has heavier members and is less complicated in pattern. The pergola must be built with a strong framework because it makes a heavier statement than an arbor. Thus proportions must be thought out ahead of time (drawn on paper). The pergola must have enough headroom for a person to walk under plus space for plants on top that are trailing downward; it must be wide enough for two people to walk abreast.

Pergola and archway posts should be 4 × 4s placed 6 or 8 feet on center to support the main framework; 3 × 4s can be used for the transverse beams above. Always anchor posts to concrete piers that are set into a concrete footing. (See Drawing 3.)

Arched Trellis

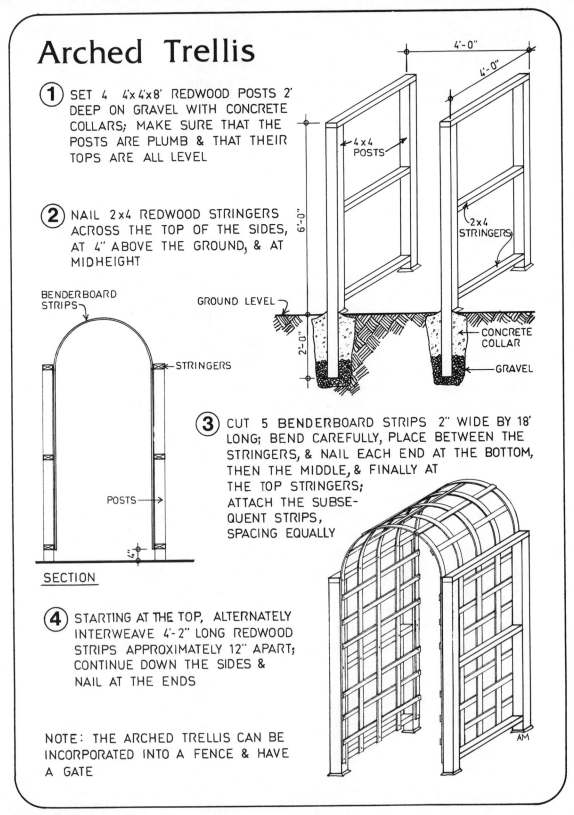

1 SET 4 4'x4'x8' REDWOOD POSTS 2' DEEP ON GRAVEL WITH CONCRETE COLLARS; MAKE SURE THAT THE POSTS ARE PLUMB & THAT THEIR TOPS ARE ALL LEVEL

2 NAIL 2x4 REDWOOD STRINGERS ACROSS THE TOP OF THE SIDES, AT 4" ABOVE THE GROUND, & AT MIDHEIGHT

BENDERBOARD STRIPS

STRINGERS

4'-0"

4'-0"

4x4 POSTS

2x4 STRINGERS

6'-0"

GROUND LEVEL

2'-0"

CONCRETE COLLAR

GRAVEL

POSTS

4"

SECTION

3 CUT 5 BENDERBOARD STRIPS 2" WIDE BY 18' LONG; BEND CAREFULLY, PLACE BETWEEN THE STRINGERS, & NAIL EACH END AT THE BOTTOM, THEN THE MIDDLE, & FINALLY AT THE TOP STRINGERS; ATTACH THE SUBSE- QUENT STRIPS, SPACING EQUALLY

4 STARTING AT THE TOP, ALTERNATELY INTERWEAVE 4'-2" LONG REDWOOD STRIPS APPROXIMATELY 12" APART; CONTINUE DOWN THE SIDES & NAIL AT THE ENDS

NOTE: THE ARCHED TRELLIS CAN BE INCORPORATED INTO A FENCE & HAVE A GATE

AM

Building an . . .

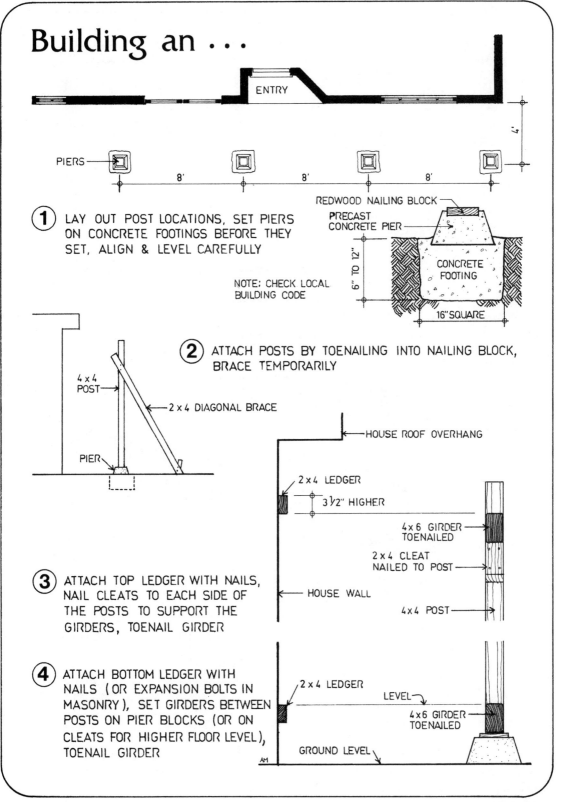

ENTRY

PIERS

8'   8'   8'

1 LAY OUT POST LOCATIONS, SET PIERS ON CONCRETE FOOTINGS BEFORE THEY SET, ALIGN & LEVEL CAREFULLY

NOTE: CHECK LOCAL BUILDING CODE

REDWOOD NAILING BLOCK

PRECAST CONCRETE PIER

6" TO 12"

CONCRETE FOOTING

16" SQUARE

2 ATTACH POSTS BY TOENAILING INTO NAILING BLOCK, BRACE TEMPORARILY

4 x 4 POST

2 x 4 DIAGONAL BRACE

PIER

HOUSE ROOF OVERHANG

2 x 4 LEDGER

3½" HIGHER

4 x 6 GIRDER TOENAILED

2 x 4 CLEAT NAILED TO POST

HOUSE WALL

4 x 4 POST

3 ATTACH TOP LEDGER WITH NAILS, NAIL CLEATS TO EACH SIDE OF THE POSTS TO SUPPORT THE GIRDERS, TOENAIL GIRDER

4 ATTACH BOTTOM LEDGER WITH NAILS (OR EXPANSION BOLTS IN MASONRY), SET GIRDERS BETWEEN POSTS ON PIER BLOCKS (OR ON CLEATS FOR HIGHER FLOOR LEVEL), TOENAIL GIRDER

2 x 4 LEDGER

LEVEL

4 x 6 GIRDER TOENAILED

GROUND LEVEL

AM

DRAWING 3

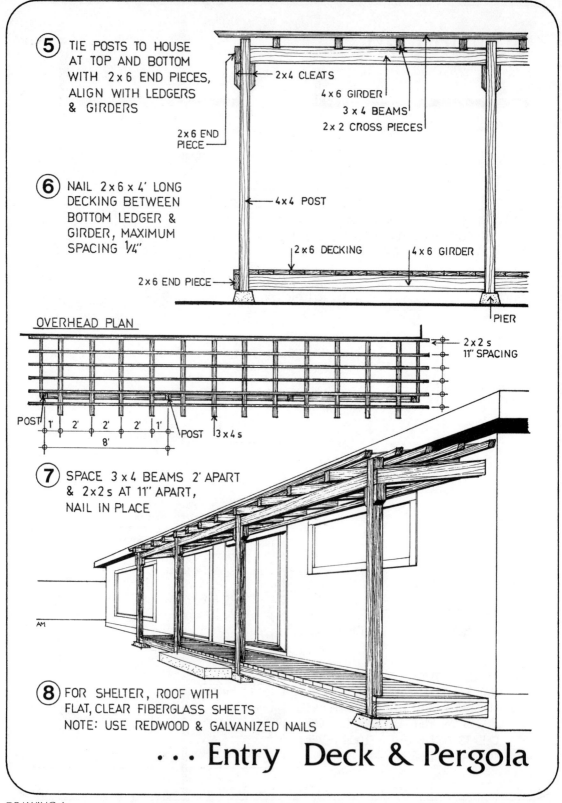

5 TIE POSTS TO HOUSE
AT TOP AND BOTTOM
WITH 2 x 6 END PIECES,
ALIGN WITH LEDGERS
& GIRDERS

2 x 4 CLEATS

4 x 6 GIRDER
3 x 4 BEAMS
2 x 2 CROSS PIECES

2 x 6 END
PIECE

6 NAIL 2 x 6 x 4' LONG
DECKING BETWEEN
BOTTOM LEDGER &
GIRDER, MAXIMUM
SPACING ¼"

4 x 4 POST

2 x 6 DECKING   4 x 6 GIRDER

2 x 6 END PIECE

PIER

OVERHEAD PLAN

2 x 2 s
11" SPACING

POST 1' 2' 2' 2' 1'   POST   3 x 4 s
            8'

7 SPACE 3 x 4 BEAMS 2' APART
& 2 x 2 s AT 11" APART,
NAIL IN PLACE

8 FOR SHELTER, ROOF WITH
FLAT, CLEAR FIBERGLASS SHEETS
NOTE: USE REDWOOD & GALVANIZED NAILS

··· Entry Deck & Pergola

Here we see the beginning of the pergola-type entrance; note that two posts have been added and the platform built. All is clean and simple.

A close-up of detail work of above photograph.

The finished entrance with the garden nook added to the left to further enhance the total picture. Now the house has a sense of entrance, a welcome look.

The garden corner adjoining the pergola; acts as a privacy barrier and adds dimension to front of house.

The length of the pergola can vary, but it should never be confined; a 4-foot pergola simply will not look right. Pergolas need a length of at least 6 feet, although 10 feet is better so they can perform their functions as entranceways.

See Drawings 3 and 4 for a step-by-step working plan of a pergola. This plan incorporates a deck and gives the house a handsome appearance. The roofing used on the pergola is optional; it serves as protection from sun and rain.

The archway, arbor, and the pergola are distinctive ways of adding beauty to your home; they impart a nostalgia to the total plan.

Construction Language

Benderboard: Thin flexible redwood veneer.

Cleat: Metal hardware usually U shaped applied to wood to support another piece of wood.

Girder: Heavy beam of wood used as a support and supported by columns.

Ledger: Strip of lumber.

Nailing block: A strip of wood attached to a surface to provide means of attaching another member by nailing.

Pier: Column of masonry.

Toenailing: Nailing at an angle.

Doors and Windows 5

Historically, doors and windows have been of many styles. Unfortunately, today's designs are so severe and simple that doors and windows have practically no character or craftsmanship. Yet these two necessary elements of a home provide the easiest way of restoring some beauty and style. Doors are not just doors, and windows are not just vacant eyes. With some ornamentation and remodeling they can come alive and contribute to the home's overall charm. For example, doors and windows can have flat lintels if the distance to be spanned is small; they can have arched heads if the distance is greater. Greek openings are defined by the lintel, Roman by the lintel and the arch, Gothic by the pointed arch, and Renaissance by the lintel and round arch. Adapting some of these classical lines to today's openings will give your house the distinct and appealing character that may be missing.

The classical Greek and Roman opening is rectangular and consists of jambs and a flat head framed with flat or molded caps or cornices. The faces of the jambs and the lintels provide surfaces that can be decorated to accent the opening. These small touches—the moldings—can create an extravagant door, a beauty to see. (We cover moldings for doors, windows, walls, and so on in Chapter X.) By breaking the molding at the top, that is, by extending it beyond the door on each side at the top, you can achieve dimension and stability. The classical openings can assume many decorative accents, depending on your skill and just how fancy you want to get.

Arched openings, hardly seen in today's architecture but very handsome, are composed of the pier, impost cap, and archivolt. The tops of the arches are heavily detailed and framed and can be decorated in many ways. It is embellishment upon embellishment, which today, of course, would look foolish, but *some* of the details can be used to create unique entrances.

The Gothic openings are somewhat more refined and narrower in structure than the Greek and Roman ones, but they are still quite ornate. They are perpendicular and more in scale with things than the large Romanesque arched doorways and windows.

The Renaissance opening perhaps has had the most influence on today's architecture; its basic elements are adapted from the Greek and Roman styles. Gothic openings have the Roman pilasters, columns, and arches, but they are refined by triangular shaped lintels and rounded arches above the doors or windows.

This is only a glimpse at the past treatment of doors and windows. Much of this is no longer used today, but some of it certainly deserves a place in your home. We have stripped windows and doors of any detailing until they now look sterile; it is time to pay some attention to the eyes and ears of a building and to create more individual effects for our homes—for ourselves and for visitors.

Doors

Doors are, of course, a means of entering a house or room, but remember that most of the time they are seen closed. Too many people forget that a door creates an impression. Think for a moment about doors you have seen; you remember those, perhaps, that had stained-glass highlights, those that were hand carved, and others that also had character.

This handsome arched door gives an entrance character; it is a paneled door with a look-through window.

An elegant Gothic-type door—in keeping with the look of the house. It is a door that denotes strength and elegance.

So what you want for your home is a handsome door, not just the stock doors sold at mills.

WOOD DOORS

There is an incredible variety of wood doors, and each type of door has a certain character. Interior doors are available with one panel or as many as fifteen panels; arrangement of the panels varies. The more panels, the more ornate the door. Just what type you should use depends on the other house appointments. A three-paneled door is always handsome, and the six-paneled colonial-type door has a warm feeling. The fifteen-paneled door is more elaborate but attractive in bigger homes. The unequal-panel door—two large panels, with a small panel in the center, for example— also has a place in today's home, although it is not as nice looking as an equal-multipaneled door.

Entrance (exterior) doors may be paneled, have glass sections, or be a combination of paneling and glass. The designs vary, from equal panels to four or six panels at the bottom and three or four top panels of glass. Or the door may have a diamond pattern at the top and bottom (four triangles that form a rectangle).

The paneled exterior door tends to give a formal look to a house. It is a substantial door that says what is inside the house or room is substantial as well. A paneled door with a bas-relief effect can take on many variations. What you select is dictated by what you can find. Try to find old doors at wrecking companies and salvage stores. Old doors are thicker, wider, and last years longer than today's standard milled door because they were made better.

If you cannot find old doors, you can buy the old-looking doors manufacturers sell. (I should warn you that these doors are expensive.) Shop carefully and always buy a door that is at least 2 inches thick; a heavier door not only looks better but it feels better when you open it. And do not get carried away by an overly elaborate door. A simple pattern may look more elegant than a complicated one.

GLASS DOORS

The beautiful glass doors of yesteryear are once again appearing in homes. These doors have beveled glass panes set in moulions; four stained glass panes, with the other panes being clear glass; or etched glass panes. A solid wood door with glass sidelights is another variation. Any glass door has a European flavor and is usually oversized. The eight-, ten-, or twelve-paned glass French door with wood mullions is quite popular and provides just enough glass, not too much. French doors are rich looking and beautiful. (We discuss how to hang French doors in the installation section further on in the chapter.)

Look for old doors at salvage places. If the glass is broken, buy the door anyway because you can always have the glass replaced with a pattern of your own choice (glazing a door is not that hard). Beveled glass panels are hard but not impossible to find; several glass companies now stock them or can order them for you. Stained-glass doors are sold at antique shops. They are expensive, so you might want to make your own stained glass. With new products like foil-simulated lead and epoxies, making stained glass is well within the average person's scope.

If you live in an area where burglary is a problem, forget glass doors. You'll be heartbroken (and house broken) if a thief knocks out a pane so he can try to reach inside for a spring lock.

HAND-HEWED DOORS

You can, if you have carpentry experience, make your own hand-hewed door by adding simple braces, carving, or so on to a new door or by buying an old door and redoing it. The beauty of the hand-carved door speaks for itself, and some interesting designs and carvings can be fashioned.

If you have never done wood carving, here is a chance to try it and create your own distinctive door. There are several books on wood carving to help you. However, do use a heavy, thick solid-core door.

INSTALLATION

Putting a door in place or hanging it was once a complicated job, but not today. If proper stud framing exists, hanging the door should not take

This beautiful hand-carved door would make any home appealing. Originally an old door, it was sandblasted to its natural look.

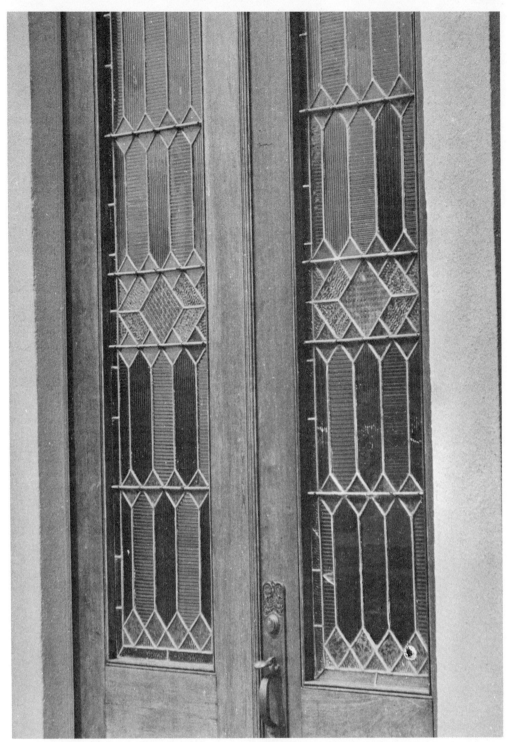

A leaded glass door is distinctive and adds great charm to a home. This entrance door is handsome indeed.

Doors can be attractive with sidelights of leaded glass as shown here. These are available at various antique stores or you can make your own stained-glass decorations.

more than an hour. The prehung doorframe is like a box with a door hinged to it. This lets you slip the box into a stud-framed opening and secure it easily. Each prehung frame has two side jambs and a head jamb dadoed together at the top. The doorstop or the molding runs around the inside of the jambs, and a sill and threshold are needed at the base of the two side jambs. The sill slopes away from the door base to keep out water.

The frame usually comes with hinges attached and the doorstop molding tacked to the frame. Pull out the hinge pins and remove the door before putting the frame in place.

For cutting a new door into an old wall, lay out the location and the measurement of the door. First, mark the line where the top of the new door header will meet the cut-off ends of old wall studs. This indicates the top line for cutting through wall coverings and determines where to cut the old studs. Figure this line by adding the header width plus 1/2 inch for shimming between the frame head jamb and the header; then add the door frame's height.

The sides, top, and bottom of the rough opening for a door should be fitted with a strip of roofing felt or any other type of insulation to act as weather stripping.

The framing for a door must be absolutely square. Once the full-length studs are positioned, line up your trimmer studs' framing. Then install the header, usually a 4-×-4-inch piece of wood. Its length is the distance between the two existing full-length studs nearest the outside of each trimmer. Cut away the soleplate so it is flush with the full-length studs. Now figure the length of the trimmer studs; they extend from the floor to the base of the headers. Tack one trimmer against the inside of each full-length stud into the headers' ends, and toenail the cut-off full-length studs into the top of the header. Nail the outer trimmers in place (into the studs).

To adjust the door frame to the proper width, place another trimmer out from one side parallel to the other trimmer stud and allow 1/2 inch on each side for shimming. Nail that trimmer into block; toenail to soleplate and headers. Weather-strip all sides and the threshold.

To replace a prehung frame within an existing opening, be sure the door frame is plumb and level at all times. (Follow Drawing 5 for this entire procedure.) The stud opening is somewhat larger than the size of the

Replacing a Door

(1) REMOVE THE EXISTING DOOR, LEAVING THE HINGES ON THE JAMB (OR REPLACE THEM)

(2) MEASURE THE OPENING — THE DOOR SHOULD CLEAR 1/16" AT SIDES & TOP & 1/2" AT BOTTOM. IF THE REPLACEMENT DOOR IS

    A. TOO BIG: CUT DOWN OR PLANE THE EDGES

    B. TOO SMALL: GLUE EQUAL WOOD STRIPS TO THE ENDS

WOOD STRIP   DOOR   WOOD STRIP

(3) SHIM THE DOOR IN PLACE, & USING THE HINGE LEAVES AS TEMPLATES, MARK & MORTISE THE DOOR, THEN SECURE THE HINGE LEAVES

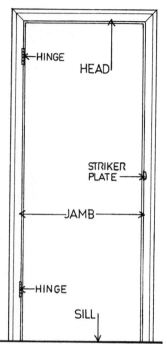

HINGE

HEAD

STRIKER PLATE

JAMB

HINGE

SILL

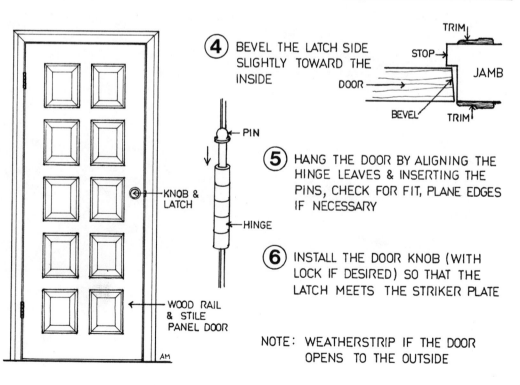

(4) BEVEL THE LATCH SIDE SLIGHTLY TOWARD THE INSIDE

TRIM

STOP

DOOR

JAMB

BEVEL

TRIM

PIN

KNOB & LATCH

HINGE

WOOD RAIL & STILE PANEL DOOR

(5) HANG THE DOOR BY ALIGNING THE HINGE LEAVES & INSERTING THE PINS, CHECK FOR FIT, PLANE EDGES IF NECESSARY

(6) INSTALL THE DOOR KNOB (WITH LOCK IF DESIRED) SO THAT THE LATCH MEETS THE STRIKER PLATE

NOTE: WEATHERSTRIP IF THE DOOR OPENS TO THE OUTSIDE

Here are some old doors found at salvage and wrecking yards being sandblasted. The equipment is rented.

These salvaged doors are wooden; the decorative effect is ironwork and the look is impressive. You can still find such doors at salvage yards.

prehung frame to allow for shimming. To shim, drive a pair of shingles into each side of the frame between the trimmer studs and the jamb, to form a tight rectangular wedge. After the frame is nailed in place, cut off the shim flush with the studs.

To position the door, center the frame in the opening from side to side and back to front; then shim the door to the estimated side clearance and fasten with stop moldings. Put shingles next to the upper hinge, and tap them together so the side of the jamb is plumb. Shim, check the plumb, and nail halfway between top and bottom shims. Now fasten the door into position with hinge pins, and shim and nail the latch side of the door

The original door to the house; it is an inexpensive hollow core door without much charm.

This paneled door was used; it is thick, solid-core and was painted after sand-blasting was done.

This photograph shows what a recessed door entry can achieve for a home; it creates an intimate come-hither look. It gives the visitor an introduction to the house, gradually leading him into the interior.

frame, always keeping a 1/16-inch clearance between the door edge and frame. Nail the door sill and threshold in place.

The doorknob and lock should be placed 36 to 38 inches above the floor. Drill for the knob and lock, carefully following the manufacturer's directions for attaching the lock. After the doorknob is secured, mark the top and bottom of the latch where it hits the frame. Position the latch's striker plate, and cut out the mortise for the latch.

The finishing touches are the doorstop molding and casing. Nail stops flush with the face of the closed door. Now nail casing trim around the opening to both the trimmer studs and the frame edges.

FRENCH DOORS

Frame up an opening for French doors (in pairs) by placing a 4-×-6-inch header and cripple studs as shown in Drawing 6. Put in 2 × 4 trimmers and the studs and sole plate. Allow for the doorframe (usually 3 1/2

French Doors

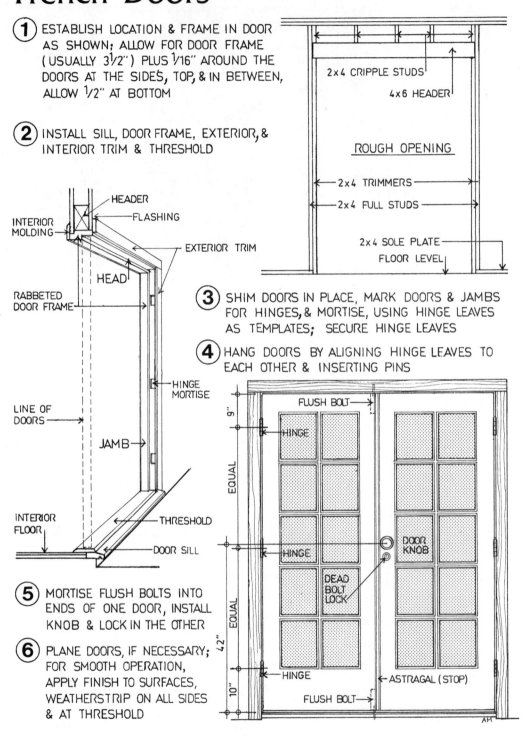

1 ESTABLISH LOCATION & FRAME IN DOOR AS SHOWN; ALLOW FOR DOOR FRAME (USUALLY 3½") PLUS 1/16" AROUND THE DOORS AT THE SIDES, TOP, & IN BETWEEN, ALLOW ½" AT BOTTOM

2 INSTALL SILL, DOOR FRAME, EXTERIOR, & INTERIOR TRIM & THRESHOLD

3 SHIM DOORS IN PLACE, MARK DOORS & JAMBS FOR HINGES, & MORTISE, USING HINGE LEAVES AS TEMPLATES; SECURE HINGE LEAVES

4 HANG DOORS BY ALIGNING HINGE LEAVES TO EACH OTHER & INSERTING PINS

5 MORTISE FLUSH BOLTS INTO ENDS OF ONE DOOR, INSTALL KNOB & LOCK IN THE OTHER

6 PLANE DOORS, IF NECESSARY; FOR SMOOTH OPERATION, APPLY FINISH TO SURFACES, WEATHERSTRIP ON ALL SIDES & AT THRESHOLD

Labels (rough opening drawing): 2x4 CRIPPLE STUDS · 4x6 HEADER · ROUGH OPENING · 2x4 TRIMMERS · 2x4 FULL STUDS · 2x4 SOLE PLATE · FLOOR LEVEL

Labels (frame detail): HEADER · FLASHING · INTERIOR MOLDING · EXTERIOR TRIM · HEAD · RABBETED DOOR FRAME · LINE OF DOORS · JAMB · HINGE MORTISE · INTERIOR FLOOR · THRESHOLD · DOOR SILL

Labels (doors drawing): FLUSH BOLT · HINGE · 9" · EQUAL · DOOR KNOB · DEAD BOLT LOCK · EQUAL · 42" · 10" · HINGE · ASTRAGAL (STOP) · FLUSH BOLT

AM

Recessed Door

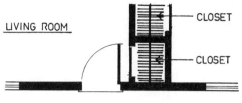

LIVING ROOM

CLOSET

CLOSET

ORIGINAL PLAN

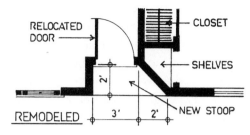

RELOCATED DOOR

CLOSET

SHELVES

NEW STOOP

2'

3'

2'

REMODELED

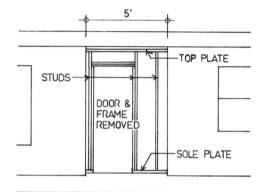

5'

STUDS

DOOR & FRAME REMOVED

TOP PLATE

SOLE PLATE

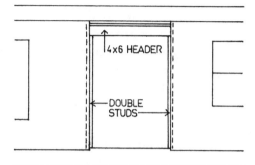

4x6 HEADER

DOUBLE STUDS

(1) REMOVE THE DOOR, FRAME, & WALL SIDING TO THE DESIRED WIDTH, THEN REMOVE THE STUDS & SOLE PLATE, BUT NOT THE TOP PLATE

(2) INSERT 2x4 STUDS AT THE ENDS, THEN SUPPORT THE HEADER WITH A SECOND 2x4 AT THE ENDS, NAIL TOGETHER

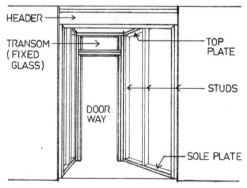

HEADER

TRANSOM (FIXED GLASS)

TOP PLATE

STUDS

DOOR WAY

SOLE PLATE

(3) BUILD THE INSIDE WALLS & DOOR FRAME WITH 2x4s, INSULATE WALLS & SHEATH TO MATCH EXISTING WALL

(4) INSTALL TRANSOM WINDOW, DOOR FRAME, & DOOR; TRIM WITH 1x3s

inches), and also allow 1/16 inch around the doors at the sides, top, and between. Leave 1/2 inch at the bottom. Shim doors in place; mark doors and jambs for hinges, and mortise them, using hinge leaves as templates. Hang doors by aligning hinge leaves to each other and inserting pins. Mortise flush bolts into the ends of the door, and install the knob and lock into the other end. If necessary, plane the doors so they are smooth and even. Weather-strip all sides and the threshold.

RECESSED DOORS

A recessed door is a clever way of creating dimension and providing an interesting entrance to a home. The door is set back providing a small corridor effect, which makes the entrance intimate. A door positioned in this manner eliminates the need for a visitor to walk directly into a room. There is a sense of entrance, and although the remodeled entranceway still has the door opening on the room, the outside entry provides an illusion of entrance. The entryway can also provide an L-shaped corner in the room, again creating charm. (See Drawing 7.)

Windows

Windows are the eyes of a house—you look out of them and people look into them—so windows deserve more thought than they are usually given. Just as you can tell a lot about people by their eyes, you also can tell a great deal about a house by its windows. Too often windows are cold steel or aluminum stock-sized items installed where necessary without advanced planning. But to make a house a home, windows should have character. I need to cite only one prime example: In Drawing 8 notice the difference between the casement window and the standard aluminum sliding window. Which window has character? The casement, of course. Casement windows invariably add charm to a home because they break up the space into small units, which creates dimension and design. The eye has something to see rather than a blank stare. Thus, select windows carefully; look for those with the character that can help, not hinder, the attitude of a house.

Windows

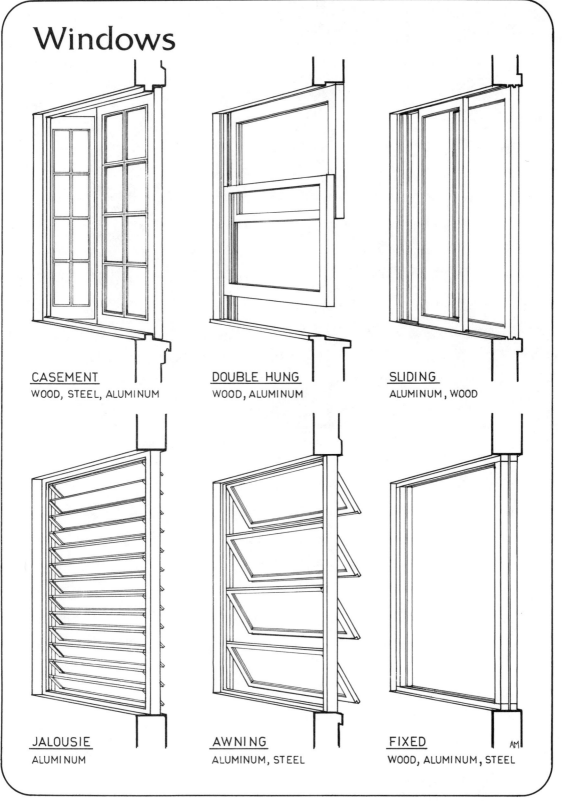

CASEMENT
WOOD, STEEL, ALUMINUM

DOUBLE HUNG
WOOD, ALUMINUM

SLIDING
ALUMINUM, WOOD

JALOUSIE
ALUMINUM

AWNING
ALUMINUM, STEEL

FIXED
WOOD, ALUMINUM, STEEL

The bay window breaks the dull line of a wall and creates eye interest; the three-sided window has infinitely more charm than a single flat window.

Another lovely bay window

These windows may be small but they still have character because of the diamond patterns.

In addition to adding character, windows, of course, allow light to enter and air to come into a room. Just where you place windows depends on your own personal preference—most people like a light room so they position windows accordingly, facing south or east. Some people want a room that is somewhat dark—so windows are set on the north side (a bedroom would be an example). Also to be considered in window placement is climate. In cold climates more windows should be oriented to the south to benefit from the heat of the sun. In mild climates northern and eastern exposures avoid the heat of the sun.

Cross ventilation is a blessing in hot weather; so when placing windows take into account this theory, which simply means air that moves across the room. Before air conditioning, windows were the only source of ventilation, so if you want to save on energy and cost it is wise to place windows to obtain the best air circulation. High windows and corner windows are not in this position. Locate windows that will take advantage of prevailing winds but not prevailing storms. (Heating costs will rise if you have a window wall where winter storms hit most frequently.)

In general, construct windows to relate to the character of the house, and place them to let the desired amount of air and light into the room.

Kinds of Windows

There are actually hundreds of types of windows and it sometimes is a dilemma to select the appropriate ones for the home. Generally, look for a window that has some character and will add to the tone of the house. I prefer a multilighted window. (In the glass trade, a "light" is designated as a single piece of glass.) The small pane effect is always attractive and fits into almost any home, from Victorian to contemporary. Sliding windows (horizontal sliders) seem sterile to me and pivoting or hopper-type windows, although they have their uses, are not very handsome.

So, in essence, the multipaned window—whether it be four lights or sixteen—is quite handsome in almost any situation. Double-hung and dormer-type windows are attractive too.

Fixed windows that do not open are often used in today's houses, and we will discuss these as well.

In most regions of the country, windows are bought ready-made (sometimes called "setup" windows). They come with sash (the frame that holds the glass), jamb (the top and side members), casing (the outside frame), and a sill (the bottom member). Other parts include stops, weather stripping. Most setup windows are made of pressure-treated lumber which means they have a wood preservative to resist moisture.

Decide on the size and shape of the window first because the rough opening must be cut to accommodate the units. You can order windows almost any jamb thickness but it must relate to the thickness of the wall. For example, most walls are made of 2 × 4s (3 1/2 inches wide) and 1/2-inch sheathing on the outside and 1/2-inch wallboard on the inside. This totals 4 1/2 inches.

CASEMENT WINDOWS

Wood casement windows come in a variety of patterns, but usually they have 8-×-12-inch glass panes divided by wooden mullions. The more panels of glass in a window, the more charm it will have. The larger the span of casement windows, the more character; casement windows rarely look good singly or in a distance less than 8 feet wide because it is the repeated pattern that give the windows their personalities. Casement windows are available in dozens of sizes and with rectangular or diamond-shaped panes.

DORMER AND DOUBLE-HUNG WINDOWS

The dormer window, popular because of its handsome shape, is essentially a casement window enclosed in a dormer frame, giving a pleasing shadow box effect. The header and sill jut out, but the window itself is recessed; this provides both dimension and detailing.

The workhorse window of yesteryear was the double-hung window: two windows one above the other, double hung. As a functional window it cannot be beat and comes in four standard types: (1) two panes, one top and one bottom, (2) one pane below and two panes above, (3) one solid

The existing window in the house; it is monotonous and without any flair.

Here salvaged windows are being installed where the original blank-looking window existed. Note insulation in walls.

pane at the bottom and four panes at the top, or (4) four panes each, top and bottom.

INSTALLATION

Let us suppose that the present windows in your home just do not do anything for the building. Your home needs some character, and the old French doors you found would give that character if they were used as windows. How to install the doors? Where to put the doors for maximum effect? How to replace any window? First, determine if the wall you want the windows on is load bearing. Any exterior wall or interior one at right angles to the ceiling joists is usually considered a load-bearing wall.

Now that you have the right wall, remove existing sash, frame, and trim and interior wall sheathing. (Follow Drawing 9 for this discussion.) Add 3 inches, and set full length studs here. Cut two 2 × 4s to measure the height of the rough opening. These studs support the header (generally two 2 × 6s nailed together with 16d nails). (Nails are discussed in Chapter 2.) Use a spacer of 3/8-inch plywood to make equal thickness to the width of the 2 × 4s.

Nail the two full length studs to the header; use 16d nails. The header itself is connected to the top plate by two 2 × 4s.

Occasionally, with different ceiling heights, the header fits snug against the bottom of the top plate so no connecting studs are necessary. Headers are of the same size unless the window is extra wide.

If the window is 3 to 5 feet wide, use 2 × 8s; if the window is over 6 feet, use 2 × 10s; and so on. Nail a 2 × 4 between the supporting studs at the height of the bottom of the window's rough opening. Nail short studs on 16-inch centers, and support this crosspiece or sill of the rough opening. Toenail the sill to the supporting studs with 10d nails; face-nail the studs with 16d nails. Toenail the studs (or cripples) to the plate with 10d nails.

FIXED ARCHED WINDOW

An arched window is hard to find at suppliers, but occasionally you may find an old church window, as I did at a salvage outlet. I felt the graceful

The finished window

How to Replace · · ·

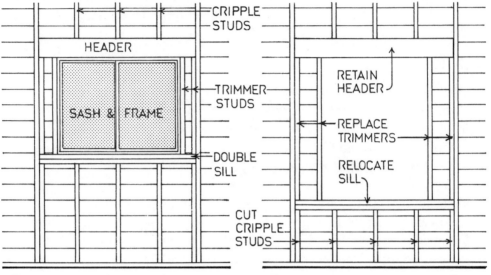

CRIPPLE STUDS

HEADER

TRIMMER STUDS

SASH & FRAME

DOUBLE SILL

RETAIN HEADER

REPLACE TRIMMERS

RELOCATE SILL

CUT CRIPPLE STUDS

① REMOVE THE SASH, WINDOW FRAME, & TRIM, & INTERIOR WALL SHEATHING

② RE-FRAME OPENING; ALLOW $3/8''$ ON ALL SIDES OF NEW WINDOW. REPAIR EXTERIOR SIDING

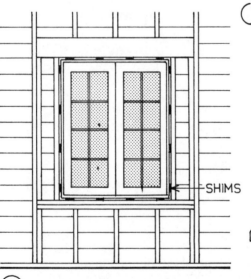

SHIMS

③ SHIM & LEVEL NEW FRAME & SASH; REPAIR INTERIOR WALL SHEATHING; ADD TRIM

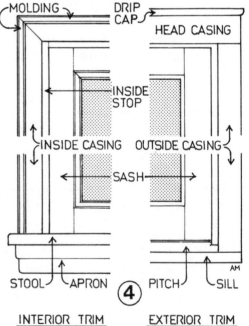

MOLDING

DRIP CAP

HEAD CASING

INSIDE STOP

INSIDE CASING   OUTSIDE CASING

SASH

STOOL   APRON

PITCH   SILL

AM

④

INTERIOR TRIM   EXTERIOR TRIM

· · · a Window

curve of the window frame and the general attitude of the window itself would add character to the kitchen area, and it did. Thus, I am adding some details here about installing an arched window. If you use bender-board (which is available at lumberyards), you can do the window installation without too much trouble.

The installation of the arched window follows the same procedure as for any window. Install the header and the frame opening, allowing for the jamb thickness plus 1/8-inch space for the top and sides. Drawing 10 shows a typical fixed arch window installation.

BAY WINDOWS

One bay window can add beauty to any plain home and its construction, although somewhat more complicated than a standard window, is not overpowering. The bay window, like most other types of windows, can be purchased as a unit and comes complete with sash in jamb and casing so much of the work is done for you. It is ready to insert into a rough-framed opening. You can also make your own bay window if you want something more distinctive and something that requires a bit more work. The work is worth the effort because it results in a unique look.

To install a bay window, first determine the size and location of the bay. Then start the foundation work for the window; this entails a suitable concrete foundation that, if possible, should join the existing foundation of the house. A concrete footing is necessary to support the foundation. Check with local building codes to determine the frost line and depth of the footing. Excavate and make level the ground for the footing. Use rented forms from rent-it companies and pour the footing and foundation. Be sure to install necessary tie rods and reinforcing rods. When the concrete foundation is ready, you can remove the siding; cut the siding as wide as the outside dimension of the foundation wall and as high as the ceiling. Now remove the interior wall, the studs, and sole plate, but do not remove the top plate. Nail in place 2-×-4-inch full studs on each side running top to bottom between the sole- and top plates. Nail trimmer studs to the full studs; these support the header. Check with local building codes for exact size of the header. Be sure to put in the cripple studs above the header to support the top plate.

Fixed Arched Window

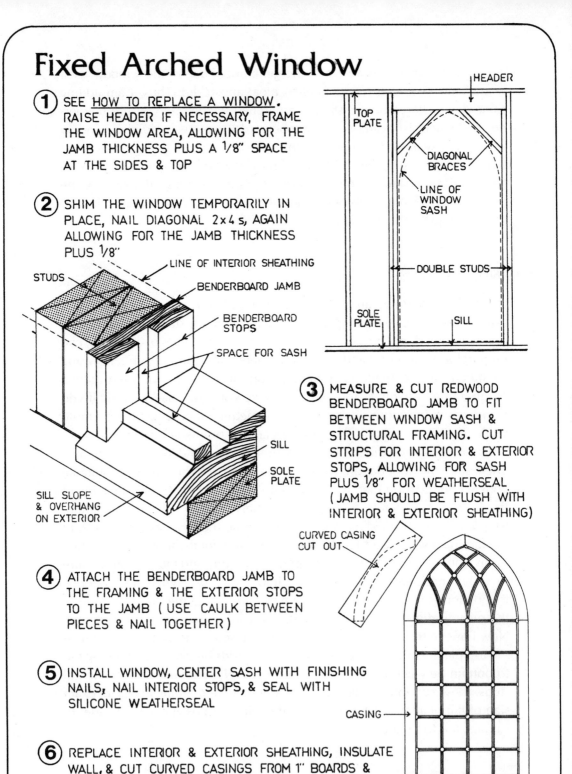

1 SEE <u>HOW TO REPLACE A WINDOW</u>. RAISE HEADER IF NECESSARY, FRAME THE WINDOW AREA, ALLOWING FOR THE JAMB THICKNESS PLUS A 1/8" SPACE AT THE SIDES & TOP

2 SHIM THE WINDOW TEMPORARILY IN PLACE, NAIL DIAGONAL 2x4 s, AGAIN ALLOWING FOR THE JAMB THICKNESS PLUS 1/8"

HEADER

TOP PLATE

DIAGONAL BRACES

LINE OF WINDOW SASH

DOUBLE STUDS

SOLE PLATE

SILL

LINE OF INTERIOR SHEATHING

STUDS

BENDERBOARD JAMB

BENDERBOARD STOPS

SPACE FOR SASH

SILL

SOLE PLATE

SILL SLOPE & OVERHANG ON EXTERIOR

3 MEASURE & CUT REDWOOD BENDERBOARD JAMB TO FIT BETWEEN WINDOW SASH & STRUCTURAL FRAMING. CUT STRIPS FOR INTERIOR & EXTERIOR STOPS, ALLOWING FOR SASH PLUS 1/8" FOR WEATHERSEAL (JAMB SHOULD BE FLUSH WITH INTERIOR & EXTERIOR SHEATHING)

CURVED CASING CUT OUT

4 ATTACH THE BENDERBOARD JAMB TO THE FRAMING & THE EXTERIOR STOPS TO THE JAMB (USE CAULK BETWEEN PIECES & NAIL TOGETHER)

5 INSTALL WINDOW, CENTER SASH WITH FINISHING NAILS, NAIL INTERIOR STOPS, & SEAL WITH SILICONE WEATHERSEAL

CASING

6 REPLACE INTERIOR & EXTERIOR SHEATHING, INSULATE WALL, & CUT CURVED CASINGS FROM 1" BOARDS & MATCH TO STRAIGHT LOWER CASINGS

A mudsill is necessary for the window so use a 2-×-4-inch board bolted to the foundation. Now remove the blocking at the existing floor joists and put in new joists as shown in step 4 of Drawing 11. Install the new plywood subfloor and a 2-×-4-inch soleplate at the outside edge.

It is now time to frame in the bay using 2-×-4-inch studs and trimmers; finish at the top with a double 2-×-4-inch top plate. To make the union with the house roof, install 2 × 4 rafters and ceiling joists; add a ledger on the house and the top plate. Matching the exterior finish of the existing house wall and also finishing the bay with siding that matches the house walls will complete the project.

Flashing and trimming are the final steps; the flashing is the metal stripping to prevent leaks and the trim is standard molding. Install the windows as shown on Drawing 12 and then do the painting and staining to match existing surfaces.

Glass

In our remodeling we deal with flat glass—sheets of glass for windows and skylights. A little knowledge about glass can help you work better with it and know what to look for when shopping.

WINDOW AND SHEET GLASS

Flat glass comes in several thicknesses and qualities, much like lumber. Very thin glass is 1/64 inch thick; very thick glass is 1 inch thick. The glass we use in windows is 1/16 or 1/8 inch thick and comes in two grades: A-glass, with little or no flaws, and B- or commercial glass, which has some small marks or seeds—not exceeding 1/32 inch long—in the glass.

Standard window glass (sold at hardware and glass stores) is an imperfect product. It is a rolled glass and inherently has flaws. That is, it is poured in a liquid state and sent through rollers to obtain its thickness and flatness. Thus window glass called SSA or SSB (1/16 inch thick) and DSA and DSB (1/8 inch thick) always has some waves in it since it has gone through a roller process.

Adding a · · ·

1 ESTABLISH THE SIZE & LOCATION OF THE BAY ON THE INTERIOR & EXTERIOR. POUR A CONCRETE FOUNDATION SIMILAR TO THE ONE EXISTING, & TIE INTO IT WITH STEEL TIE RODS (CONSULT LOCAL BUILDING CODES)

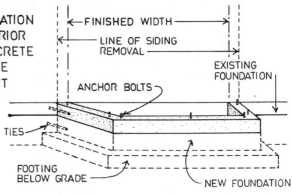

FINISHED WIDTH

LINE OF SIDING REMOVAL

EXISTING FOUNDATION

ANCHOR BOLTS

TIES

FOOTING BELOW GRADE

NEW FOUNDATION

TOP PLATE

FULL STUD

CRIPPLE STUDS

HEADER

TRIMMER STUDS

6'-9"

EXISTING FLOOR

MUDSILL

JOISTS

CRAWL SPACE

NEW FOUNDATION

2 CUT & REMOVE THE SIDING AS WIDE AS THE OUTSIDE DIMENSION OF THE FOUNDATION & AS HIGH AS THE CEILING. REMOVE THE INTERIOR SHEATHING, THE STUDS, & SOLE PLATE, BUT NOT THE TOP PLATE (SEE HOW TO REMOVE A WALL)

3 INSTALL 2x4 FULL-HEIGHT STUDS BETWEEN THE SOLE & TOP PLATES; NAIL WITH 2x4x6'-9" TRIMMER STUDS TO SUPPORT A HEADER AT BOTH ENDS OF THE OPENING, NAIL THE HEADER IN PLACE (CONSULT CODES FOR SIZE). ADD 2x4 CRIPPLE STUDS ABOVE, TO SUPPORT THE TOP PLATE

NOTE: THE OPENING MAY BE TEMPORARILY SEALED WITH PLYWOOD SHEETS ON THE INTERIOR SIDE

4 BOLT A 2x4 REDWOOD MUDSILL TO THE FOUNDATION, REMOVE THE BLOCKING AT THE EXISTING FLOOR JOISTS, & ATTACH NEW JOISTS, OVERLAPPED 6", FROM THE EXISTING SILL TO THE NEW SILL. ADD NEW BLOCKING AT THE ENDS & PROVIDE AIR VENTS THROUGH THE BLOCKING, AS REQUIRED BY THE CODES

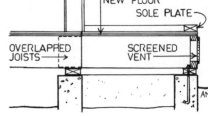

NEW FLOOR

SOLE PLATE

OVERLAPPED JOISTS

SCREENED VENT

AM

5 NAIL A PLYWOOD SUBFLOOR SO THAT THE NEW FLOOR LEVEL MATCHES THE EXISTING FLOOR (SHIM, IF NECESSARY). THEN NAIL A 2x4 SOLE PLATE AT THE OUTSIDE EDGE

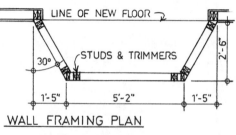

WALL FRAMING PLAN

6 FRAME IN THE BAY WITH 2×4 STUDS & TRIMMERS TO SUPPORT THE HEADERS OVER THE WINDOWS; FRAME THE WINDOWS, DEPENDING UPON THE SIZE. FINISH AT THE TOP WITH A DOUBLE 2×4 TOP PLATE. ATTACH THE FRAMING TO THE HOUSE WITH LAG SCREWS

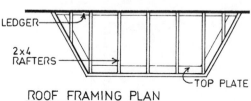

ROOF FRAMING PLAN

7 FRAME THE ROOF WITH 2×4 RAFTERS & CEILING JOISTS, ATTACH ON A LEDGER AT THE HOUSE & THE TOP PLATE; SHEATH WITH 5/8" EXTERIOR PLYWOOD & ROOF SIMILAR TO THE HOUSE

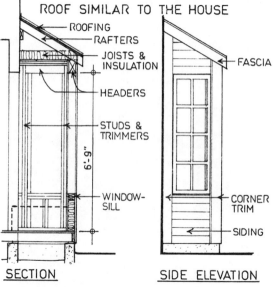

SECTION **SIDE ELEVATION**

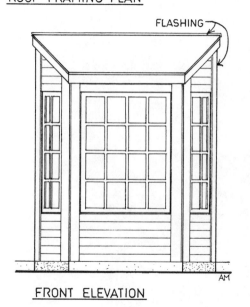

FRONT ELEVATION

8 ENCLOSE THE BAY WITH SIDING TO MATCH THE HOUSE; FLASH & TRIM AT THE CORNERS, INSULATE THE CEILING & WALLS (SEE <u>INSULATING CEILINGS</u>; & <u>INSULATING WALLS</u>) THEN SHEATH THE INTERIOR WALLS & CEILING AS DESIRED, & INSTALL INTERIOR MOLDING

9 INSTALL WINDOWS (SEE <u>HOW TO REPLACE A WINDOW</u>); TRIM THE WINDOW FRAMES INSIDE & OUT, PAINT &/OR STAIN THE INTERIOR & EXTERIOR SURFACES & TRIM, FINISH THE FLOOR TO MATCH THE EXISTING, OR IN-STALL A FIXED WINDOW SEAT

... Bay Window

The finished window.
Because they were available, French doors are used as windows here; the rough opening is being framed.

The completed windows, as seen from the inside.

A close-up of a French door used as the window.

The original windows in the back of our house; one is an old-fashioned double-hung; the other a small casement. Both were removed and replaced with more suitable windows.

Window glass comes in boxes of 50 or 100 square feet, in sizes from 8 × 10 inches to 36 × 60 inches. Glass is priced on the even inch, and since you do not want too many sheets, you will probably buy glass by the piece. It pays to buy stock sizes (even inch) rather than having it cut to a specific size of say 8 1/2 × 10 1/4 (unless a specific size is necessary) because you would pay for 10 × 12 inches.

The glass you buy will have clean-cut edges, with no protection against sharpness. So always specify glass with seamed or ground edges so the sharpness will be removed.

Also called sheet glass is crystal glass, which designates glass 3/16 and 7/32 inch thick. The heavier the glass, the less apt it is to break, and for some panels the heavier glass is a wise choice. Crystal glass is more expensive than window glass, but small pieces, say, 10 × 20 inches, are relatively inexpensive. Again, like window glass crystal glass should be bought on the even inch for economy. Also, ground or seamed edges should be specified.

POLISHED PLATE GLASS

Polished plate glass is essentially glass polished on both surfaces by huge buffer wheels so all waviness is eliminated. This glass is 24 percent more costly than window and sheet glass, but it is perfect if you want a very fine window. Polished plate glass is available in 1/8- and 1/4-inch thicknesses. As with other glass it should be ordered on the even inch, with all edges seamed or ground.

STAINED GLASS

Stained glass is also called cathedral glass, or antique glass, in the trade. It is translucent colored glass, with ripples or mounds on one surface and the other surface smooth, or with both surfaces textured. Cathedral glass is slightly thicker than standard SSB window glass and is cut in the same manner as window glass. This glass costs twice as much as clear glass; it is sold at glass stores and crafts shops.

CUTTING GLASS

Cutting glass with a glass cutter is actually a simple process if you score or fracture the glass only when making the cut. The fracture causes the glass molecules to separate along the line being scored. The secret of using the inexpensive glass cutter (available at hardware stores) is the amount of pressure applied. The pressure must be uniformly applied and neither too heavy nor too light. The next important trick is to break the glass immediately before the separated molecules heal themselves.

To actually break the glass, place a long pencil or strip of wood underneath the score line. Then press down with the palms of each hand, one palm on each side of the cut, to apply enough (but not too much) pressure. The impact of the palms on the glass breaks it along a clean-cut line.

To cut glass, be sure the glass is clean; wash it with detergent, rinse it with warm water, and dry thoroughly. Set the glass pane on a level table protected with an old carpet or bath towel. Hold the cutter almost perpendicular and dip it into oil; get a small dab of oil on the cutting wheel. For a straight cut, place the cutter about 1/32 inch from the edge of the glass (to avoid edge chipping), and make a firm continuous cut without lifting the cutter. You will know if you are doing it properly because the cutter on the glass makes a smooth and even sound. As soon as the glass is scored, place the wooden pencil directly under the score line, and immediately place your thumbs or palms on each side of the line. Apply pressure; the glass will separate. If the glass does not break, use the end of the cutter and tap gently along the scored line. You should see a fracture develop along the line. Then apply equal pressure to the two sides of the fracture line and snap the glass apart.

Shaped pieces of glass—curves, arcs—require more expertise. For these, cardboard patterns are necessary; place them on the glass, and then apply the score line as you would for straight cuts. To separate a thin glass strip from a wider piece, use a glass pliers. Grasp the narrow side of the glass with the pliers and the other side with your hand, and snap off the small piece with the pliers. Corners or slight projections can be nipped off with the indented part of the glass cutter or with flat-nosed pliers.

No matter what kind of glass you are using or what kind of cut is being made, you must follow certain safety precautions. Sharp edges of glass will cut you, so wear an old pair of household gloves. Avoid grasping or holding glass by its edges because you will be cut. Always keep your body and feet at a safe distance from the cutting table, and never cut glass close to your face. If you are reasonably careful, few accidents will happen.

The thinner the glass, the easier it is to cut. If you are cutting glass 3/16 or 1/4 inch thick, do it only after you have experience in glass cutting. And if the idea of cutting glass frightens you altogether (although it should not), buy glass already cut at stores.

The stained glass window is a focal point of this room. It is a fixed window and creates a handsome effect.

Construction Language

Beam: A horizontal timber used for support.

Bevel: Angle cut on piece of wood.

Blocking: Small piece of 2-×-4-inch lumber.

Cripple studs: Vertical 2-×-4s above and below window openings.

Flashing: Sheet metal set where roof meets a wall; acts as weatherproofing.

Footing: Concrete platform installed below frost line.

Foundation: Wall, usually masonry.

Full-height studs: Vertical 2 × 4 running from floor to ceiling.

Header: A beam or board set at right angle to floor joists to form opening for a door or window.

Jamb: Side and top frame of a window or door.

Joist: A space between two wooden members.

Lagscrew: Special screw for plaster installation.

Lintel: Horizontal member spanning and usually carrying a load above an opening.

Mortise: A slot cut into wood to receive another piece of wood.

Mudsill: Base plate at bottom of window and doors, usually 2 × 6 laid flat.

Mullion: Vertical divider between window panes.

Rafter: A beam that supports a roof.

Sheathing: Exterior surface of wall.

Shims: Tapered pieces of wood.

Shingles: Red or white cedar sawn to a taper.

Sole plate: Bottom horizontal board, usually 2 × 6 at floor line.

Stud: Vertical member, usually 2 × 4 used in framing.

Subfloor: Rough plywood; on top of this finished floor is laid.

Tie rods: Rod used as a connecting member.

Top plate: Horizontal board doubled; usually 2 × 6 above door and window opening supporting second floor joists or roof rafters.

Trimmer stud: Vertical members on sides of window and door openings.

Walls | 6

If you are remodeling a house, you will find that there is always a wall which, if removed, would open up two areas and double the space both visually and physically. Whether you remove the wall completely (which is okay if the wall is not load bearing) or remove the wall and replace it with charming posts or pilasters, you open a whole new dimension in a house. If you want to be even more ornamental, and if the house demands it, you might think about archways—an old-fashioned feature that makes a home inviting.

Removing a Wall

It is tougher to remove a wall than to put up the columns or posts—so be prepared to use some muscle. First, determine whether the wall is load bearing. Any exterior or interior wall that is at right angles to the ceiling joists is usually considered a bearing wall. When you remove a wall you must install a suitable header to hold the weight of the room above it; an opening width of 4 to 6 feet requires a 4 × 6 header, a 6- to 8-foot opening requires a 4 × 8 header, and a 10-foot opening requires a 4 × 10 header. A width.over 10 feet increases the size of the necessary header to 4 × 14. Since you will be handling large header timbers, get some help from friends or relatives; and order the header at least 2 feet longer than the length of the opening. (You can trim the header after determining the exact stud spacing.) Because the floor load above (or roofing, if there is no floor) requires support, be sure you know exactly what you are doing. Once the wall is removed, you will need supports while you ready the window, opening, posts, or other structural elements. Use floor jacks or temporary bracing to hold the wall while work is in progress.

Look at Drawings 13 and 14 which show how to remove a bearing wall and a nonbearing wall, respectively. Removing a wall is not an insurmountable task if you do it easily and slowly. To get the opening started, with a power or keyhole saw cut into the wall where you want the opening; when the opening is large enough, use a crosscut saw. If the wall is gypsum or lath board, you can saw without too much damage to surrounding surfaces. Expose enough of the framing so you can install a new header and trimmer studs. Remove the wall with a crowbar, or if the opening is small, use the claw end of a hammer, prying gently but firmly.

If the wall is plaster, use the claw end of the hammer to chop out a horizontal ribbon of plaster between two laths as close as possible to the outline of the desired opening. Then, with a cold chisel and hammer, chop away 4 to 6 inches of plaster inside the vertical lines to expose the lathing. Saw through the lathing as closely as possible to a stud.

If you are removing an exterior wall for a new window opening, you might run into stucco and wire construction. Here you must use muscle power and smash the stucco with a hammer or hatchet to expose the chicken wire; cut the wire with tin snips, and then pull away the old sections from the sheathing. The easiest way to approach the stucco exterior wall is to use a power masonry saw, which allows you to saw through the stucco and wire at the same time. Wear leather gloves and protective goggles for this project.

If the exterior wall is wood siding, all you need is a power saw and hammer.

In most cases wall repairing will entail installing new studs or replastering to seal and cover your tear-out. These are not difficult jobs; in fact, the patch-up is fun. Patch up with wood, plaster, or whatever the situation calls for. With wood, just cut out replacement pieces the size of the area to be covered, nail the pieces in place, and finish with a molding. With plaster, build up the surface of the torn opening a little at a time and smooth the plaster into place.

Insulating Walls

Insulating a wall is really an easy process. In fact, it is so easy that it is usually overlooked; but insulation saves heat in the winter and keeps houses cool in the summer. Generally, only exterior walls are insulated. Insulation (and there are several types available, with the sleeve-type, aluminum foil rock wool the most popular) involves placing the insulation padding within the studs and stapling it in place. If loose-fill insulation is used, it is generally blown into place. If your walls are masonry, apply board or sheet insulation to the interior side, and then apply wall finish over the insulation.

Drawing 15 contains insulation data. Always check local building codes for the minimum amount of insulation required.

Posts and Columns

Posts and columns (and pilasters) are old-fashioned decorations that add a spot of elegance. For example, two 4 × 4 posts separating a space can simultaneously enlarge the area and create two separate units with each space evoking a different mood. Just where you position the posts or columns depends on the total amount of space; in a given area of 15 × 30 feet, set the two columns equidistant in the room, each column in parallel alighment 2 feet from the 30-foot wall. Thus there is 11 feet between the columns.

How to Remove · · ·

(1) DETERMINE IF THE WALL IS LOAD-BEARING OR NON-BEARING

A. IF THE CEILING JOISTS ARE AT RIGHT ANGLES TO THE WALL, THE WALL IS SUPPORTING THE CEILING JOISTS & IS LOAD-BEARING, THE WALL WILL HAVE TO BE REPLACED WITH A SUPPORTING BEAM & POSTS AT BOTH ENDS

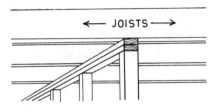

B IF THE CEILING JOISTS ARE PARALLEL TO THE WALL & IF THERE ISN'T A WALL DIRECTLY ABOVE ON A SECOND FLOOR THE WALL IS NON-BEARING & CAN BE SAFELY REMOVED

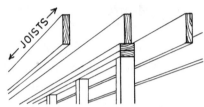

DOUBLE TOP PLATE

STUDS

SOLE PLATE

(2) REMOVE ANY DOORS, ALL MOLDING & THE WALL SHEATHING ON BOTH SIDES, RELOCATE ANY ELECTRICAL WIRING

(3) IF THE WALL IS NON-BEARING REMOVE THE STUDS, SOLE PLATE & TOP PLATE, PATCH THE WALLS CEILING & FLOOR TO MATCH THE EXISTING SURFACES

(4) IF THE WALL IS LOAD-BEARING CONSULT LOCAL BUILDING CODES FOR THE SIZE OF THE BEAM REQUIRED TO SUPPORT THE CEILING JOISTS, BUILD TEMPORARY SUPPORTING WALLS 3' FROM EACH SIDE OF THE WALL TO BE REMOVED USING 2x4 STUDS 24" ON CENTER, A 2x4 SOLE PLATE & TOP PLATE

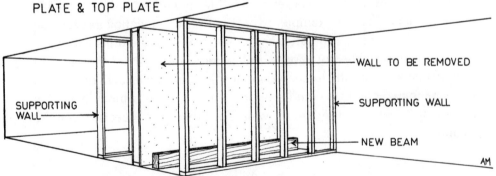

WALL TO BE REMOVED

SUPPORTING WALL

SUPPORTING WALL

NEW BEAM

AM

NOTE: BE SURE THAT THE BEAM IS IN THE SPACE BETWEEN THE SUPPORTING WALLS BEFORE BUILDING THEM

⑤ REMOVE THE BEARING WALL STUDS, TOP PLATE & SOLE PLATE, THEN CAREFULLY MEASURE THE HEIGHT FROM THE FLOOR TO THE BOTTOM OF THE JOISTS, CUT 2 4x4 POSTS DEDUCTING THE HEIGHT OF THE BEAM

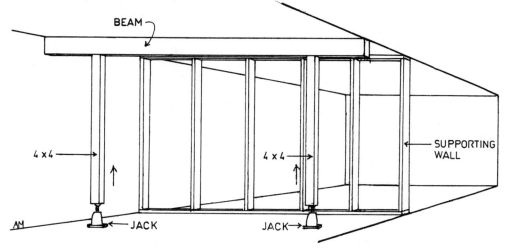

⑥ SUPPORT THE NEW BEAM IN PLACE WITH 2 4x4's ON TOP OF HOUSE JACKS, CAREFULLY ALIGN THE BEAM & RAISE IT SLIGHTLY SO THAT THE PERMANENT 4x4 POSTS CAN BE PLACED UNDER EACH END

⑦ ATTACH THE POSTS TO THE WALLS WITH LAG SCREWS OR BY TOE-NAILING; IN EITHER CASE COUNTERSINK THEM & FILL THE HOLES WITH WOOD PUTTY

⑧ LOWER THE BEAM IN PLACE, REMOVE THE 4x4's & THE JACKS, TOE-NAIL THE BEAM TO THE POSTS, THEN REMOVE THE TEMPORARY SUPPORTING WALLS

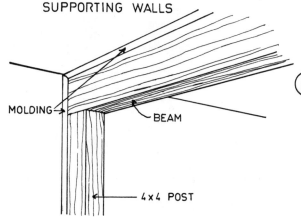

⑨ COUNTERSINK THE NAILS & FILL WITH WOOD PUTTY, PATCH THE FLOOR & WALLS AS REQUIRED, ADD MOLD-ING & FINISH WITH STAIN OR PAINT AS DESIRED

... a Wall

Insulating Walls

NOTE: USUALLY ONLY THE PERIMETER (EXTERIOR) WALLS ARE INSULATED, BUT INSULATING INTERIOR PARTITIONS CAN HELP TO CONTROL SOUND

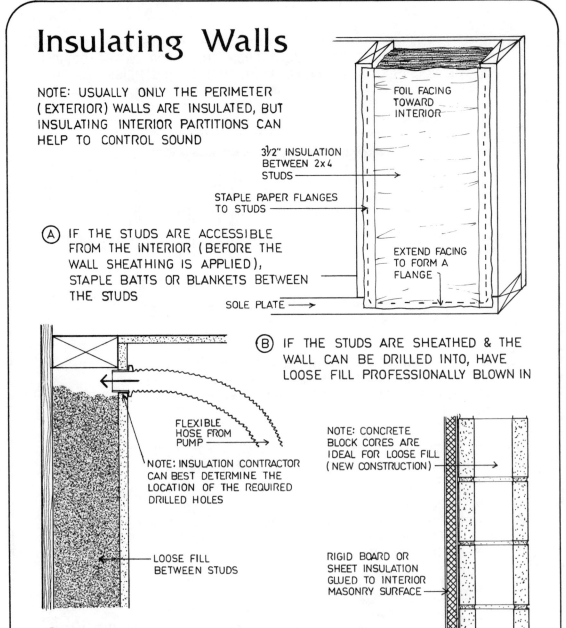

FOIL FACING TOWARD INTERIOR

3½" INSULATION BETWEEN 2x4 STUDS

STAPLE PAPER FLANGES TO STUDS

(A) IF THE STUDS ARE ACCESSIBLE FROM THE INTERIOR (BEFORE THE WALL SHEATHING IS APPLIED), STAPLE BATTS OR BLANKETS BETWEEN THE STUDS

EXTEND FACING TO FORM A FLANGE

SOLE PLATE →

(B) IF THE STUDS ARE SHEATHED & THE WALL CAN BE DRILLED INTO, HAVE LOOSE FILL PROFESSIONALLY BLOWN IN

FLEXIBLE HOSE FROM PUMP

NOTE: INSULATION CONTRACTOR CAN BEST DETERMINE THE LOCATION OF THE REQUIRED DRILLED HOLES

NOTE: CONCRETE BLOCK CORES ARE IDEAL FOR LOOSE FILL (NEW CONSTRUCTION)

LOOSE FILL BETWEEN STUDS

RIGID BOARD OR SHEET INSULATION GLUED TO INTERIOR MASONRY SURFACE

(C) IF THE WALLS ARE SOLID (MASONRY), APPLY BOARD OR SHEET INSULATION TO THE INTERIOR SIDE & APPLY WALL FINISH OVER

AM

NOTE: CHECK LOCAL BUILDING CODES FOR THE MINIMUM AMOUNT OF INSULATION THAT IS REQUIRED

Column Divider

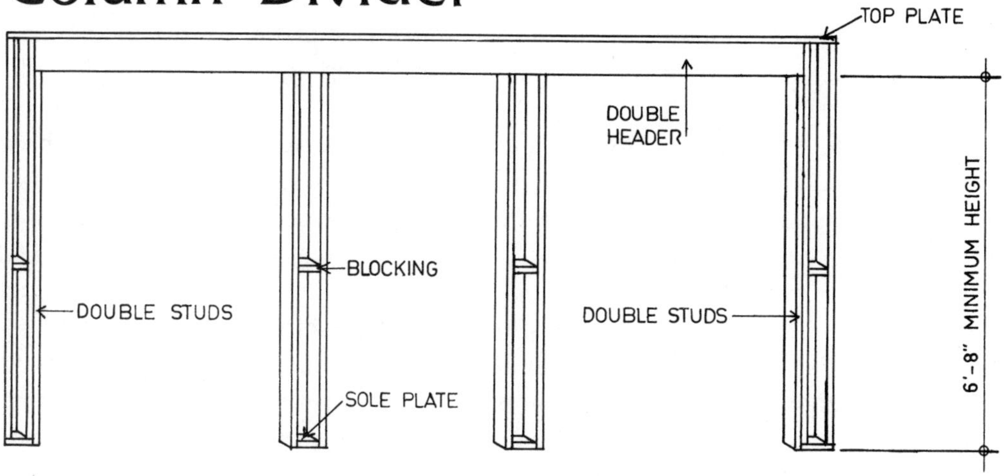
TOP PLATE
DOUBLE HEADER
BLOCKING
DOUBLE STUDS
DOUBLE STUDS
SOLE PLATE
6'-8" MINIMUM HEIGHT

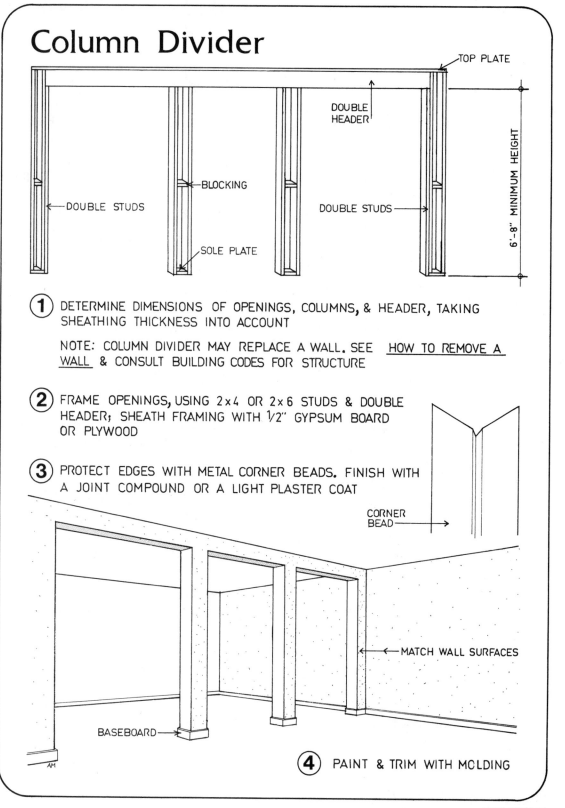

1. DETERMINE DIMENSIONS OF OPENINGS, COLUMNS, & HEADER, TAKING SHEATHING THICKNESS INTO ACCOUNT

   NOTE: COLUMN DIVIDER MAY REPLACE A WALL. SEE <u>HOW TO REMOVE A WALL</u> & CONSULT BUILDING CODES FOR STRUCTURE

2. FRAME OPENINGS, USING 2 x 4 OR 2 x 6 STUDS & DOUBLE HEADER; SHEATH FRAMING WITH 1/2" GYPSUM BOARD OR PLYWOOD

3. PROTECT EDGES WITH METAL CORNER BEADS. FINISH WITH A JOINT COMPOUND OR A LIGHT PLASTER COAT

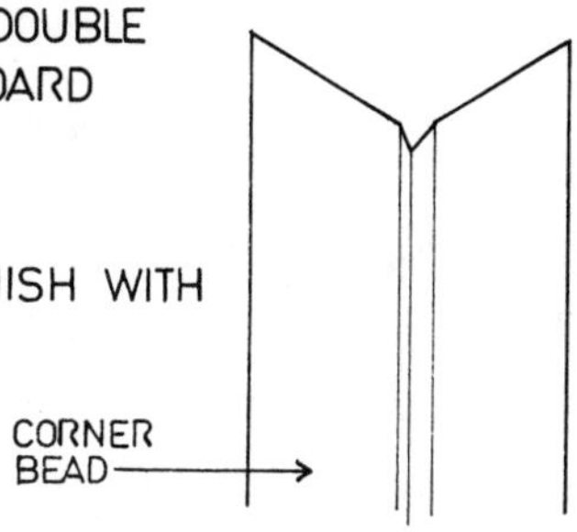
CORNER BEAD

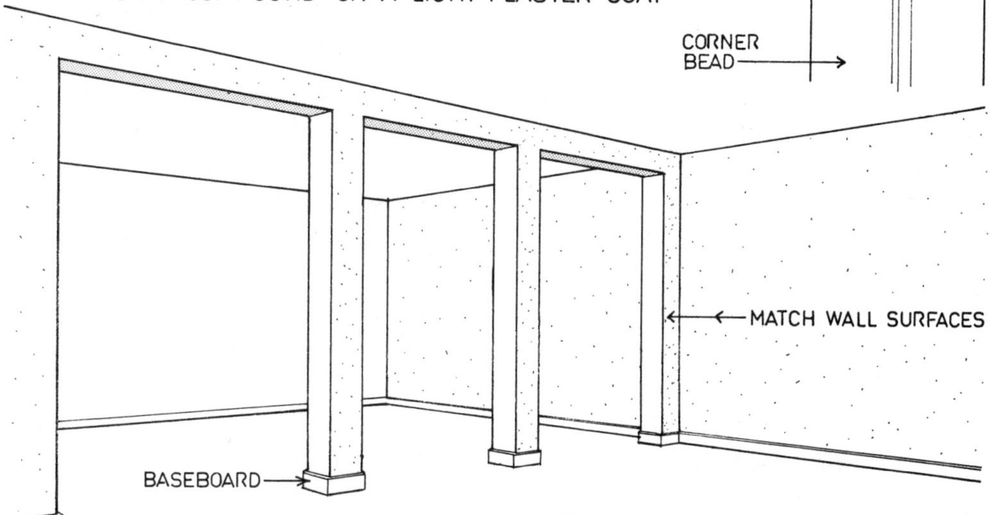
MATCH WALL SURFACES
BASEBOARD
AM

4. PAINT & TRIM WITH MOLDING

Prefabricated lightweight hollow-core posts and columns, ready for installation, are sold at lumber yards. Like platforms, these items are easy to install: they can be attached at the top and bottom with base holder clamps that attach to the floor and the post or column and ceiling clamps that fasten to the ceiling and the column or post. So if you rent a house or an apartment, you are installing only eight screws per column: four screws in the ceiling and four in the floor. When you move, you can remove the columns and putty the screw holes to avoid any problem with the landlord or manager.

You can also make your own posts by nailing double studs and headers. (See Drawing 16.) Cover the posts or columns with gypsum board or plywood; then you can apply fabric (very effective), or mirror them for a dazzling effect. Mirror blocks, sold at hardware stores and crafts shops, are self-adhesive, so you just press them in place.

The posts that separate my dining room from the living room are approximately 10 inches square (smaller sizes can be used, depending on the space involved). My total living and dining room area is 15 × 30 feet, and a two-post arrangement works well. This elegant addition costs only $20. And since I used prefab posts, it took me merely a few hours to put them in place.

Plaster Arch

The interior arch provides a graceful and flowing line, especially if posts or columns are not appropriate to the total scheme, or if rooms are boxy and sterile. By its very nature the arch requires a rather long span and can be used as an entry from one room to another, or in a series for a very spacious effect.

Drawing 17 shows a plaster arch used as an entranceway; it is framed with 2 × 4s. The arch itself is wood framed; metal lathing frames the entryway. The most difficult part of installing an arch is attaching the hardware lath to the existing wood frame. Once the arch is wood framed and covered in metal lath, you have to plaster. (If you are not familiar with plasterwork, you may want to have a professional tackle the job.) However, plastering is not that difficult to do; manufacturers offer directions on packages, and the job can be done in a few days.

Plaster Arch

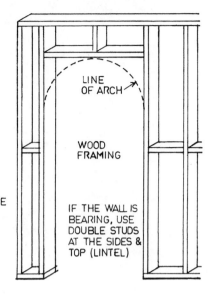

1 FRAME THE ARCH, USING 2x4 STUDS, OR FOR A THICKER ARCH, USE WIDER STUDS OR BUILD A DOUBLE, SPACED 2x4 WALL
ALLOW FOR THICKNESS OF PLASTER & LATH (5/8″ TO 3/4″)

LINE OF ARCH

WOOD FRAMING

IF THE WALL IS BEARING, USE DOUBLE STUDS AT THE SIDES & TOP (LINTEL)

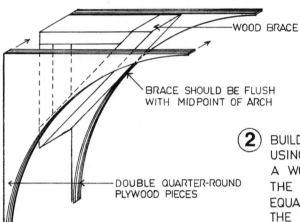

WOOD BRACE

BRACE SHOULD BE FLUSH WITH MIDPOINT OF ARCH

DOUBLE QUARTER-ROUND PLYWOOD PIECES

2 BUILD TWO QUARTER-ROUND GUSSETS, USING 1/2″ (OR THICKER) PLYWOOD & A WOOD TRIANGULAR BRACE.
THE FINISHED THICKNESS MUST EQUAL THE STUD WIDTH, NAIL TO THE FRAME

3 CUT METAL LATH & ATTACH WITH SELF-FURRING NAILS, CAREFULLY BEND & NAIL A STRIP FOR THE UNDERSIDE

4 USE A FLEXIBLE CORNER BEAD FOR THE CURVED EDGES, NAIL CAREFULLY TO THE PLYWOOD, USE A RIGID BEAD FOR THE STRAIGHT EDGES & CORNERS

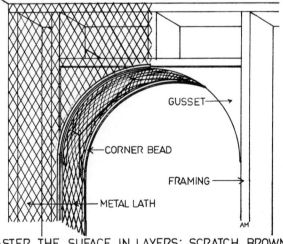

GUSSET

CORNER BEAD

FRAMING

METAL LATH

AM

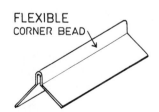

FLEXIBLE CORNER BEAD

5 PLASTER THE SUFACE IN LAYERS: SCRATCH, BROWN, & FINISH COATS (BROWN COAT MAY BE OMITTED)

NOTE: CONSULT THE MANUFACTURER OR THE GYPSUM ASSOCIATION FOR THE TYPES OF PLASTER & THE RECOMMENDED MIX & APPLICATION

The existing walls of the original house badly needed work.

Old paneling of the original house was anything but handsome; most walls were resurfaced in plaster.

Framing a wall around a window; note the insulation.

Wallboard being applied.

Wallboard plastered between joints.

Finished new wall surface; it is a plaster-type paint with texture.

The kitchen wall as it originally appeared.

The new kitchen completely revamped.

Wood Paneling

Wood paneling is available in many finishes in standard prefinished sheets and various types of veneer. Shop first before making a decision. The paneled wall usually lends itself to a library, a guest room, or some room that is not too large. Too much paneling (contrary to what manufacturers say) can make a room confining.

To panel a wall, as shown in Drawing 18, first remove the baseboard and any moldings and trim at doors and windows. In other words, strip off the existing materials. If the wall is masonry or uneven, you must fur it up with strips. Attach wood panels with adhesive or nails; the basic installation is simple once the preparation is done. When the paneling is finished, attach all moldings and trim.

DIAGONAL SIDING

Today you can perform miracles with surface wall treatment, that is, an application of siding or board. Siding is generally 3/4 inch thick, varying from 3 1/8 to 10 13/16 inches wide. (The actual dimensions of your walls will dictate the width of the siding.) Small rooms should be done in narrow siding, say, 3 1/8 inch; larger areas benefit from wider siding.

Remove any existing wall covering, and prepare the wall for the siding. When you are applying siding, it is imperative that you start right. Begin at a lower corner with a perfect 45-degree angle. Be sure all is level and flush, or the end result will be less than pleasing. Carefully measure and cut each successive board with its ends at a 45-degree angle; nail each board to studs. The last piece of wood must be pattern-cut into place as shown in Drawing 19.

If you are using tongue and groove, the first piece at the triangle should be tongue up. If you are using shiplap, the upper lap should be up. In tongue-and-groove construction the last piece must have the tongue removed for flush fitting.

If you have done the construction properly and all is even and flush, baseboard and trim should not be used because it detracts from the total pattern. However, if the construction is *not* perfect, use trim to cover errors.

Wood Paneled Wall

NOTE: PANELING IS AVAILABLE IN 4'x 8' OR 4'x10' PREFINISHED SHEETS & VARIOUS TYPES OF GROOVED OR PLAIN PLYWOOD (SUCH AS ROUGH SAWN OR FINE VENEERS)

(1) REMOVE THE BASEBOARD, ANY MOLDING & TRIM AT DOORS & WINDOWS, ETC.

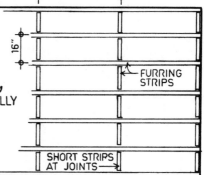

(2) IF THE WALL IS MASONRY OR IS UNEVEN, ATTACH 1x2 FURRING STRIPS HORIZONTALLY AT 16" ON CENTER (USE MASONRY NAILS). IF DAMPNESS IS A PROBLEM, STAPLE A POLYETHYLENE VAPOR BARRIER TO THE FURRING STRIPS

(3) MOVE ANY ELECTRICAL BOXES OUT TO BE FLUSH WITH THE NEW WALL SURFACE

(4) MEASURE THE WALL HEIGHT AT SEVERAL POINTS, & CUT THE PANELS ABOUT 1/4" LESS THAN THE MEASUREMENT

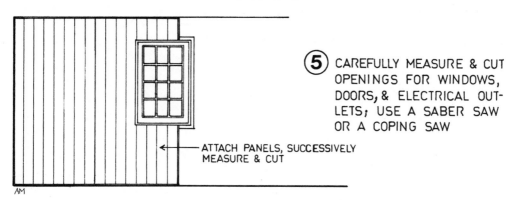

ATTACH PANELS, SUCCESSIVELY MEASURE & CUT

AM

(5) CAREFULLY MEASURE & CUT OPENINGS FOR WINDOWS, DOORS, & ELECTRICAL OUT- LETS; USE A SABER SAW OR A COPING SAW

(6) THE PANELS CAN BE ATTACHED WITH ADHESIVE &/OR NAILS. APPLY THE ADHESIVE WITH EITHER A CAULKING GUN OR WITH A NOTCHED TROWEL (FOLLOW MANUFACTURER'S DIRECTIONS). NAILS TO MATCH PANELING ARE AVAILABLE, OR COUNTERSINK FINISHING NAILS & FILL WITH MATCHING WOOD PUTTY

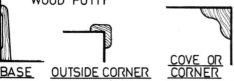

BASE   OUTSIDE CORNER   COVE OR CORNER

(7) ATTACH MATCHING MOLDING OR REFINISH THE EXISTING MOLDING & REINSTALL; COUNTERSINK NAILS & FILL WITH MATCHING WOOD PUTTY

Diagonal Siding

NOTE: SIDING IS USUALLY $\frac{3}{4}$" THICK & VARIES FROM $3\frac{1}{8}$" TO $10\frac{13}{16}$" WIDE. TONGUE & GROOVE CAN BE BLIND NAILED (CONCEALED); SHIPLAP OR OTHER JOINTS MUST BE FACE NAILED

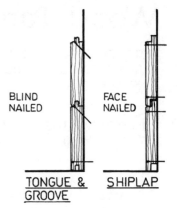

BLIND NAILED

FACE NAILED

TONGUE & GROOVE

SHIPLAP

(1) START AT A LOWER CORNER WITH A 45° TRIANGLE (OTHER ANGLES MAY BE USED). IF TONGUE & GROOVE, THE TONGUE SHOULD BE UP; IF SHIPLAP, THE UNDERLAP SHOULD BE UP

45°

FIRST PIECE

BLIND NAIL AT TONGUE

45°

90°

FACE NAILED

(2) CAREFULLY MEASURE & CUT EACH SUCCESSIVE BOARD WITH ENDS AT 45°. NAIL TO STUDS WITH FINISHING NAILS. BE SURE TO MOVE ANY ELECTRICAL BOXES OUT TO BE FLUSH WITH THE NEW WALL SURFACE

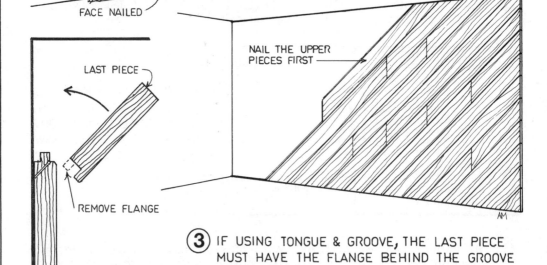

LAST PIECE

NAIL THE UPPER PIECES FIRST

REMOVE FLANGE

(3) IF USING TONGUE & GROOVE, THE LAST PIECE MUST HAVE THE FLANGE BEHIND THE GROOVE REMOVED SO THAT IT WILL FIT IN EASILY

(4) THE WOOD CAN BE STAINED (FOLLOW MANUFACTURER'S DIRECTIONS) OR LEFT NATURAL; IN EITHER CASE APPLY A CLEAR FINISH

(5) BASEBOARD & TRIM ARE NOT NECESSARY WHEN THE BOARDS HAVE BEEN EVENLY INSTALLED. COUNTERSINK THE NAILS & FILL WITH MATCHING PUTTY

Where once there was a solid wall, these two posts now support the load-bearing wall and at the same time create a handsome open look.

HORIZONTAL BENDERBOARD WALL

Redwood benderboard is very handsome, and if you want a new concept for a wall treatment, this is the answer because it is so unique. The benderboard is available in various widths. To start the application, paint the wall a dark color so if wood shrinks gaps will not be noticeable. Start at the ceiling, working down; countersink nails, and fill all holes with matching wood putty. If the wall is too wide for single board lengths, stagger the joints and nail them to the studs behind, as shown in Drawing 20.

Benderboard walls look best natural, so use a clear finish like Varathane.

Fabric Paneling

With the fabric wall you can introduce pattern to a room; there are floral prints, geometric prints, stripes—almost anything. And the fabric installation is not difficult; it must be done slowly and carefully, but certainly it is within the scope of most people. Drawing 21 will help you along.

Remove any existing wall surface, and apply 1/2-inch fiberboard. (If there are any electrical outlets or switches, cut out appropriate openings.) Cut the fabric about 6 inches longer and wider than the fiberboard panels, and center each piece of fabric on the backside of each panel. Staple from the center of each long side of fabric pulling the fabric evenly. Fold the ends of the fabric under and staple the fabric.

Attach the fabric-covered panels with finishing nails. Always countersink nails and smooth over with fabric.

Alcoves/Telephone Niches

A small alcove creates an intimate space within a room, further defines the room, and adds a personal note. The alcove is easy to construct, although it does require removal of wall sheathing and framing. (See Drawings 13 and 14: How to Remove a Wall.) You install new beams and posts, and patch the ceiling and floor. Build the new wall with 2-×-4s as

Horizontal Benderboard Wall

NOTE: REDWOOD BENDERBOARD IS AVAILABLE IN VARIOUS WIDTHS & IS
IDEAL FOR CURVED WALLS

(1) EXISTING WALL SURFACE SHOULD BE
PAINTED A DARK COLOR SINCE THE
BENDERBOARD HAS SQUARE EDGES
& MAY SHRINK, EXPOSING THE WALL
BEHIND

(2) IF THE BOARDS ARE SLIGHTLY TAPERED, NAIL WITH THE THICKER EDGE
DOWN. USE 4d (1½") FINISHING NAILS; START AT THE CEILING, WORK-
ING DOWN. COUNTERSINK THE NAILS & FILL THE HOLES WITH MATCHING
WOOD PUTTY

(3) IF THE WALL IS TOO WIDE FOR SINGLE BOARD LENGTHS, STAGGER THE
JOINTS & NAIL THEM TO THE STUDS BEHIND

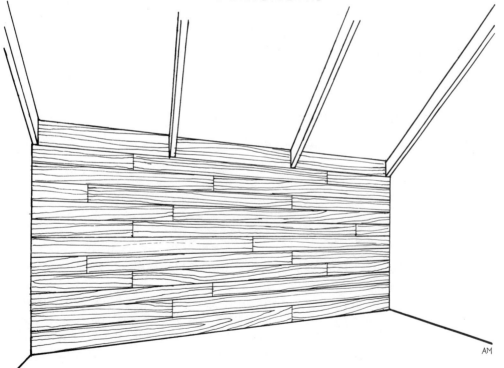

AM

(4) LEAVE THE BOARDS UNFINISHED, OR BRING OUT THE NATURAL COLOR
WITH LACQUER, VARNISH, OR A CLEAR SYNTHETIC FINISH

Fabric Paneled Wall

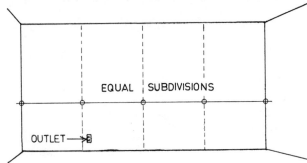

EQUAL ¦ SUBDIVISIONS

OUTLET →

NOTE: FABRIC-COVERED FIBER-
BOARD WILL PROVIDE SOUND-
PROOFING & CAN ACT AS A
FLOOR-TO-CEILING TACK BOARD

1 REMOVE THE BASEBOARD & ANY MOLDING , THEN SUBDIVIDE THE WIDTH
INTO EQUAL SECTIONS OF 4' OR LESS; CUT THE 4'x 8'x 1/2" FIBERBOARD
PANELS, MINUS 1/8" FOR THE FABRIC THICKNESS (MORE FOR HEAVIER
FABRIC)

2 IF THERE ARE ANY WALL OUTLETS OR SWITCHES, CAREFULLY MEASURE &
CUT OUT APPROPRIATE HOLES, RELOCATE THE WALL BOXES SO THEY WILL
BE FLUSH WITH THE NEW SURFACE

3 CUT THE FABRIC ABOUT 6" LONGER & WIDER
THAN THE PANELS; CENTER THE PANEL ON
THE BACKSIDE; STAPLE, STARTING FROM
THE CENTER OF EACH LONG SIDE, PULLING
THE FABRIC EVENLY & SNUGLY. FOLD THE
ENDS NEATLY LIKE A PACKAGE & STAPLE

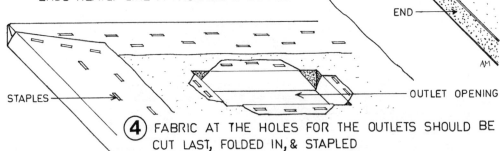

END

STAPLES

OUTLET OPENING

4 FABRIC AT THE HOLES FOR THE OUTLETS SHOULD BE
CUT LAST, FOLDED IN, & STAPLED

5 ATTACH THE PANELS WITH FINISHING NAILS WHEREVER NAILS WOULD BE
EXPOSED. CAREFULLY PART THE FIBERS OF THE FABRIC WITH THE NAIL
BEFORE NAILING IN. USE A NAILSET TO COUNTERSINK THE NAILS, & SMOOTH
OVER THE FABRIC

6 WHEN ALL THE PANELS ARE ATTACHED, REPLACE THE BASEBOARD, ANY
MOLDING & SWITCH OR OUTLET WALL PLATES

Creating . . .

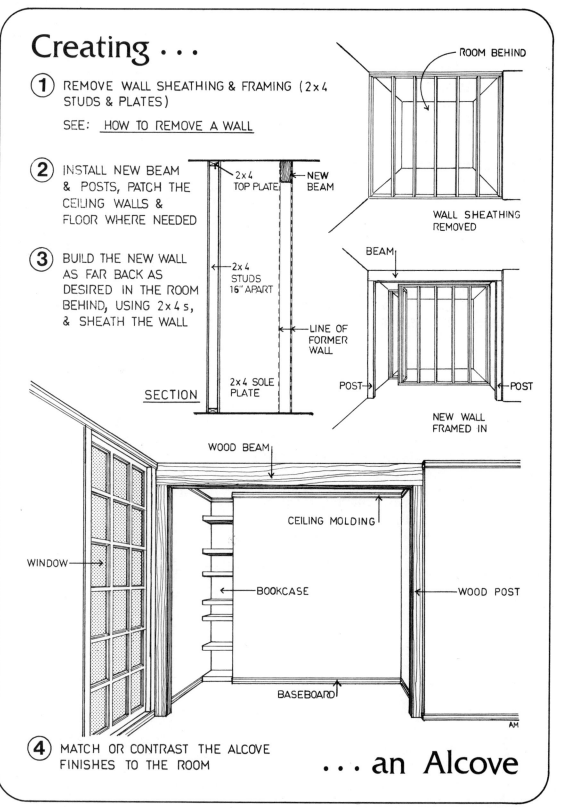

(1) REMOVE WALL SHEATHING & FRAMING (2 x 4 STUDS & PLATES)

SEE: HOW TO REMOVE A WALL

(2) INSTALL NEW BEAM & POSTS, PATCH THE CEILING WALLS & FLOOR WHERE NEEDED

(3) BUILD THE NEW WALL AS FAR BACK AS DESIRED IN THE ROOM BEHIND, USING 2 x 4 s, & SHEATH THE WALL

ROOM BEHIND

WALL SHEATHING REMOVED

2 x 4 TOP PLATE

NEW BEAM

2 x 4 STUDS 16" APART

LINE OF FORMER WALL

2 x 4 SOLE PLATE

SECTION

BEAM

POST

POST

NEW WALL FRAMED IN

WOOD BEAM

CEILING MOLDING

WINDOW

BOOKCASE

WOOD POST

BASEBOARD

(4) MATCH OR CONTRAST THE ALCOVE FINISHES TO THE ROOM

. . . an Alcove

Telephone Niche

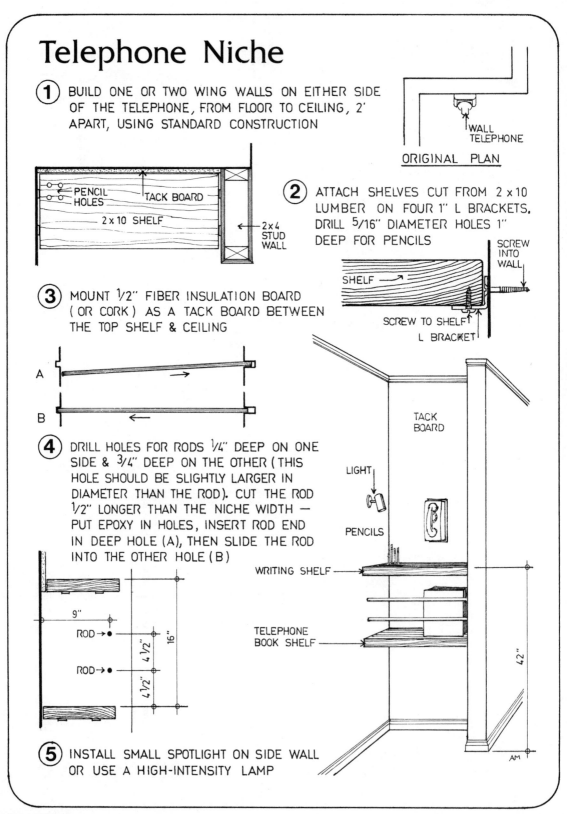

1 BUILD ONE OR TWO WING WALLS ON EITHER SIDE OF THE TELEPHONE, FROM FLOOR TO CEILING, 2' APART, USING STANDARD CONSTRUCTION

ORIGINAL PLAN

WALL TELEPHONE

PENCIL HOLES — TACK BOARD

2 x 10 SHELF

2 x 4 STUD WALL

2 ATTACH SHELVES CUT FROM 2 x 10 LUMBER ON FOUR 1" L BRACKETS. DRILL 5/16" DIAMETER HOLES 1" DEEP FOR PENCILS

SCREW INTO WALL

SHELF →

SCREW TO SHELF

L BRACKET

3 MOUNT 1/2" FIBER INSULATION BOARD (OR CORK) AS A TACK BOARD BETWEEN THE TOP SHELF & CEILING

A

B

4 DRILL HOLES FOR RODS 1/4" DEEP ON ONE SIDE & 3/4" DEEP ON THE OTHER (THIS HOLE SHOULD BE SLIGHTLY LARGER IN DIAMETER THAN THE ROD). CUT THE ROD 1/2" LONGER THAN THE NICHE WIDTH — PUT EPOXY IN HOLES, INSERT ROD END IN DEEP HOLE (A), THEN SLIDE THE ROD INTO THE OTHER HOLE (B)

TACK BOARD

LIGHT

PENCILS

9"

ROD →

ROD →

16"

4 1/2"

4 1/2"

WRITING SHELF

TELEPHONE BOOK SHELF

42"

5 INSTALL SMALL SPOTLIGHT ON SIDE WALL OR USE A HIGH-INTENSITY LAMP

AM

Framing up for an alcove.

The completed alcove.

far back as desired, and sheath the wall with fiberboard. Then match the finish of the existing walls. Drawing 22 presents an easy-to-follow plan.

A telephone niche is highly functional and gives you privacy. (See Drawing 23.) Build wing walls from floor to ceiling by using standard construction. Install shelves on L brackets. Put in cork board between the top shelf and ceiling as a place for messages. Use rods (or wooden dowels) between the bottom and top shelves to hold phone books. For the finishing touch, add a small lamp on the side wall.

Construction Language

Baseboard: A milled board nailed onto wall at floor line.

Blocking: A wooden block used as a temporary support.

Brace: A board set at an angle.

Corner bead: A piece of wood with an indentation on each side for protecting angle of wall.

Countersink: To set head of screw or nail at or below surface.

Double header: Door or window lintel made from two pieces of lumber, placed upright and nailed together.

Double studs: Double vertical supports.

Gusset: A board connecting rafters butting end to end.

Lintel: Horizontal piece of wood that supports an opening for door or window.

Metal lathing: Grid pattern metal sheet.

Polyethylene vapor barrier: Plastic sheets used to prevent moisture absorption.

Shiplap: A board with a groove to allow each board to overlap the other but with surfaces on same plane.

Soleplate: Bottom horizontal board, usually 2 × 6 at floor line.

Tongue and Groove: A board with tongue in one edge and a groove in the other.

Top plate: Horizontal board doubled, usually a 2 × 6 above door and window opening.

Wing wall: Wall built at right angle.

Skylights | 7

For too many years solid, bleak ceilings have covered our house and apartment worlds. The skylight, once used only in factory ceilings, is now popular for our living needs, and rightly so. Skylights can add more light and charm, beauty and a feeling of spaciousness to a room than any other building device. So what took them so long to become popular? Until recently there were few skylight kits available to the public (the plastic bubble skylight kit was perhaps the first one introduced), and glass skylights used to leak (although today there are excellent sealers available). After using several plastic bubble-shaped skylights, I found that my own designed and self-constructed steel-and-glass skylights looked better and lasted longer.

Besides being bubble shaped, skylights can be flat, recessed, flush, hipped, gabled, triangular, of plastic, plexiglass, glass, and so on. Skylights can go into almost any room in the home, but they are dramatically outstanding in living rooms and, to a lesser extent, in bathrooms. Whether the room has a high or a low ceiling, a skylight will create a distinctive effect: the low-ceiling room will seem taller, and the high-ceiling room will seem more dimensional and less barren. So put skylights wherever you want light and beauty, and build them yourself or if absolutely necessary, have them built. The material and design of the skylight, no matter what room the skylight is in, is of utmost importance, so for aesthetic purposes I recommend glass and wood. Glass is heavier than plastic but does not discolor or mar as acrylic or plastic tend to do. Glass is generally more difficult to install because it must be cut to a specific size and is tougher to handle than acrylic. (The plastic bubbles are more suitable in such utilitarian places as greenhouses, where they are not constantly on display.)

The skylight as a structural device requires good framing and flashing where it joins the roof to eliminate any leakage. Drawings 24 to 27 will help you considerably in making and constructing your skylight yourself and save you a good deal of money.

Opening the Roof

Installing a skylight requires removing part of the roof and suitable rough framing as previously explained. The toughest part of skylight installation is cutting the hole or space for it; the actual construction as you can see from our drawings is not that difficult. Locate the skylight on the ceiling so you will only have to cut a minimum number of joists. This involves working on a ladder and using a pry bar to remove existing roofing and ceiling materials. The mess is generally considerable so have suitable tarps on the floor. Cut the hole in the ceiling or roof with a saw; to do this, drill holes at each corner and start the cut with a keyhole saw. Once the initial cut is made, a pry bar can be used to remove roofing or ceiling material. Then joists have to be cut and roof sheathing removed. Always cut away an additional 1 1/2-inch strip of roofing around the opening for installing the curb.

Opening for a Skylight

① VERIFY THE DIMENSIONS, LOCATE THE SKYLIGHT ON THE CEILING SO THAT A MINIMUM NUMBER OF JOISTS WILL HAVE TO BE CUT. CUT THROUGH THE CEILING, ALLOWING FOR THE HEADERS (WHICH SUPPORT THE CUT JOISTS)

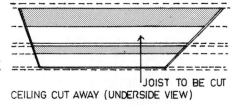

JOIST TO BE CUT

CEILING CUT AWAY (UNDERSIDE VIEW)

② CUT THE JOISTS & INSTALL THE DOUBLE HEADERS (SAME SIZE AS THE JOISTS) ON EITHER SIDE

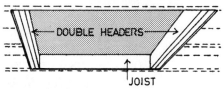

DOUBLE HEADERS

JOIST

OPENING FRAMED
(UNDERSIDE VIEW)

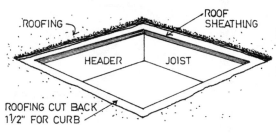

ROOFING

ROOF SHEATHING

HEADER   JOIST

ROOFING CUT BACK
1½" FOR CURB

③ CUT THROUGH THE ROOF SHEATHING & ROOFING PLUS A 1½" STRIP OF ROOFING AROUND FOR SETTING THE CURB

④ BUILD A CURB WITH 2x6s WITH THE SAME INTERIOR DIMENSIONS AS THE OPENING; MAKE SURE THAT THE CORNERS ARE SQUARE (CHECK SKYLIGHT FIT)

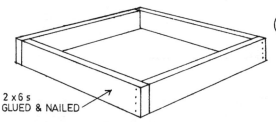

2x6s
GLUED & NAILED

⑤ PRY ROOFING UP AROUND THE EDGES. APPLY ROOF CEMENT & SLIDE FLASHING IN ON ALL SIDES (OVERLAP FLASHING)

⑥ SET THE CURB & TOENAIL IN PLACE; NAIL THE FLASHING TO THE TOP EDGE OF THE CURB

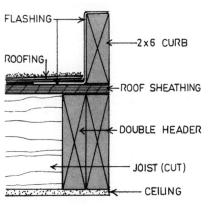

FLASHING

ROOFING

2x6 CURB

ROOF SHEATHING

DOUBLE HEADER

JOIST (CUT)

CEILING

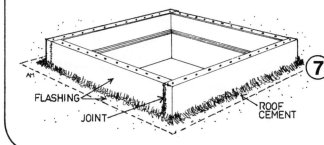

FLASHING

JOINT

ROOF
CEMENT

⑦ APPLY ROOF CEMENT LIBERALLY TO THE JUNCTION OF THE ROOFING & FLASHING, ALSO TO THE FLASHING JOINTS

Narrow & Sloped ···

1 DETERMINE SIZE OF SKYLIGHT & ANGLE OF SLOPE

    A. IF SKYLIGHT IS TO BE PARALLEL TO JOISTS, LOCATE IT BETWEEN THEM & ADD SIMILAR SIZE BLOCKING 4' ON CENTER, MAXIMUM

    B. IF PERPENDICULAR TO JOISTS, DO NOT CUT THEM, LEAVE THEM EXPOSED

2 SEE <u>OPENING FOR A SKYLIGHT</u>. BUILD UP ONE SIDE OF CURB & ADD SLOPED ENDS CUT FROM 2x 12s; USE A CANT STRIP AT LOW SIDE, INSTALL CURB, NAILING FLASHING TO SIDES, SEALING WELL

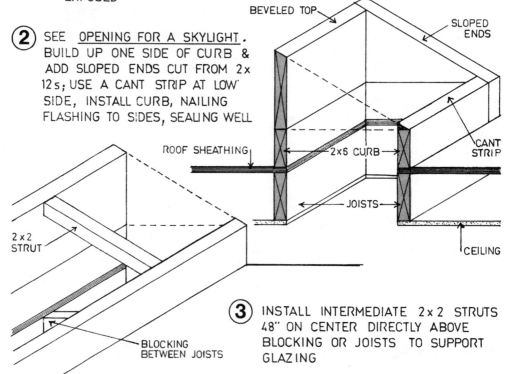

BEVELED TOP

SLOPED ENDS

ROOF SHEATHING

2x6 CURB

CANT STRIP

JOISTS

2x2 STRUT

BLOCKING BETWEEN JOISTS

CEILING

3 INSTALL INTERMEDIATE 2x2 STRUTS 48" ON CENTER DIRECTLY ABOVE BLOCKING OR JOISTS TO SUPPORT GLAZING

4 NAIL 3/8" x 3/4" BATTENS TO THE OUTSIDE EDGE OF THE TOP OF THE FRAME & CENTERED ON TOP OF STRUTS

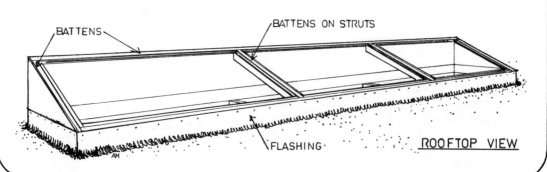

BATTENS

BATTENS ON STRUTS

FLASHING

<u>ROOFTOP VIEW</u>

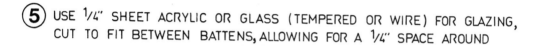

5 USE ¼" SHEET ACRYLIC OR GLASS (TEMPERED OR WIRE) FOR GLAZING, CUT TO FIT BETWEEN BATTENS, ALLOWING FOR A ¼" SPACE AROUND

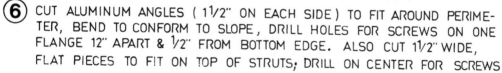

6 CUT ALUMINUM ANGLES (1½" ON EACH SIDE) TO FIT AROUND PERIMETER, BEND TO CONFORM TO SLOPE, DRILL HOLES FOR SCREWS ON ONE FLANGE 12" APART & ½" FROM BOTTOM EDGE. ALSO CUT 1½" WIDE, FLAT PIECES TO FIT ON TOP OF STRUTS; DRILL ON CENTER FOR SCREWS

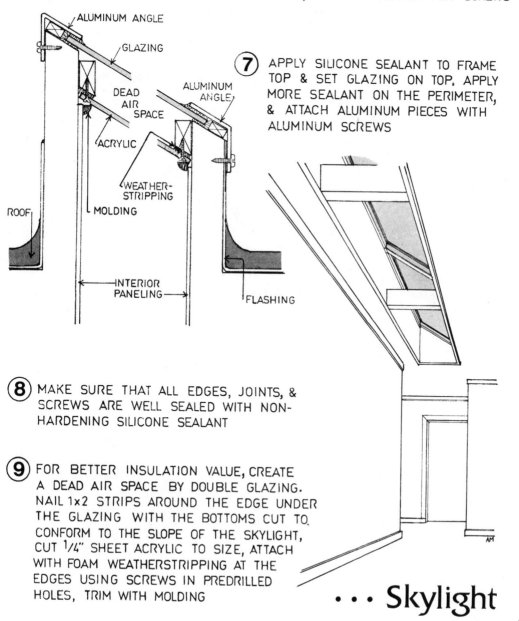

ALUMINUM ANGLE

GLAZING

DEAD AIR SPACE

ALUMINUM ANGLE

ACRYLIC

WEATHER-STRIPPING

MOLDING

ROOF

INTERIOR PANELING

FLASHING

7 APPLY SILICONE SEALANT TO FRAME TOP & SET GLAZING ON TOP. APPLY MORE SEALANT ON THE PERIMETER, & ATTACH ALUMINUM PIECES WITH ALUMINUM SCREWS

8 MAKE SURE THAT ALL EDGES, JOINTS, & SCREWS ARE WELL SEALED WITH NON-HARDENING SILICONE SEALANT

9 FOR BETTER INSULATION VALUE, CREATE A DEAD AIR SPACE BY DOUBLE GLAZING. NAIL 1x2 STRIPS AROUND THE EDGE UNDER THE GLAZING WITH THE BOTTOMS CUT TO CONFORM TO THE SLOPE OF THE SKYLIGHT, CUT ¼" SHEET ACRYLIC TO SIZE, ATTACH WITH FOAM WEATHERSTRIPPING AT THE EDGES USING SCREWS IN PREDRILLED HOLES, TRIM WITH MOLDING

... Skylight

Prefabricated Skylight

1 VERIFY CURB DIMENSIONS & INSIDE DIMENSIONS OF SKYLIGHT UNIT. TEST FIT UNIT TO CURB

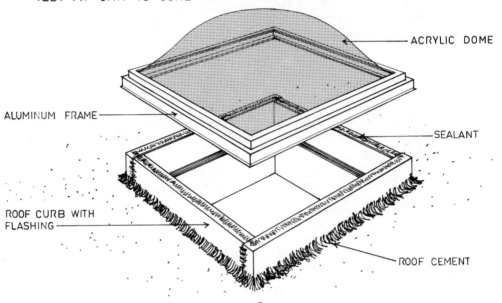

ACRYLIC DOME

ALUMINUM FRAME

SEALANT

ROOF CURB WITH FLASHING

ROOF CEMENT

2 APPLY NON-HARDENING SILICONE OR CAULKING ALL AROUND TOP OF CURB TO WEATHERSEAL UNIT

3 PLACE UNIT ON TOP OF CURB, CENTER IT, & PRESS DOWN FIRMLY

4 USE SHIMS IF NECESSARY TO KEEP UNIT FIRMLY CENTERED; SECURE TO CURB WITH ALUMINUM SCREWNAILS

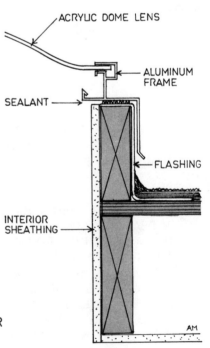

ACRYLIC DOME LENS

ALUMINUM FRAME

SEALANT

FLASHING

INTERIOR SHEATHING

AM

NOTE: DOUBLE-LENS DOMES PROVIDE BETTER INSULATION VALUE

The Skylight Opening

For skylight work you need a header, flashing, a curb, cement, glazing compounds, nails, and glass or plastic. No matter what kind of skylight you make, you will have to have a curb for it; a curb is the wood frame and is made of 2 × 6 lumber. Use highest quality redwood because the skylight frame must be straight and aligned properly to avoid leaks.

To put a skylight into an existing ceiling (follow Drawing 24), place it as I suggested, so only a minimum number of joists will have to be cut. Cut through the ceiling, allowing for the header, which supports the cut joists. Now cut the joists and install the double headers (same size as the joists) on either side of the joists. Cut through the roof sheathing and roofing, and leave a 1 1/2-inch strip for the curb to fit into. Build the curb with 2 × 6s, with the same interior dimensions as the opening. Be sure the opening is square, or you will have quite a job installing the skylight. Now, as shown in step 5 of Drawing 24, pry roofing up around the edges, slide flashing into place, and apply roof cement. Put the flashing in on all sides, and overlap it. Toenail the curb into place, and nail the flashing to the top edge of the curb. Finally, apply roof cement to the junction between the roofing and flashing.

The opening is now ready for a homemade or prefabricated skylight.

Homemade Skylights

The skylight we show in Drawings 25 and 26 is sloped; skylights should be sloped so rain can run off them, not into the home. Determine the size of the skylight and the angle of slope. If the skylight is to be parallel to joists, locate it between joists and add blocking 4 feet on centers. If the skylight is to be perpendicular to the joists, do not cut them but rather, leave them exposed.

Now follow steps 2 and 3 of Drawing 25 to slope the ends, build up the curb, and install the struts. Follow step 4 for attaching the battens. Next, install the acrylic or glass (glass is easier to clean than acrylic and does not stain). Study step 6 carefully; the aluminum angles have to fit snugly and accurately. Next, apply the silicone sealant (use a caulking gun) to the

The initial cut is made for a single skylight opening.

A crowbar is used to remove the ceiling material.

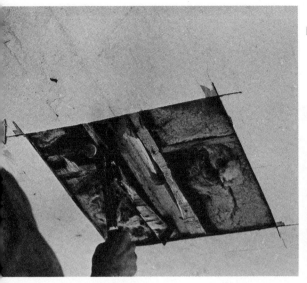

Removing the ceiling joists.

Framing the opening for the skylight.

Headers for skylight installed.

Plastic bubble skylight installed.

Completed skylight.

frame top, set the glass or acrylic panes in place (make sure the bead of silicone is higher than the batten so when you put the aluminum angle in place it meets the silicone and forms a seal), and apply more silicone to perimeter. Attach the metal pieces. Always follow step 8, or you will have a soggy mess in your room on the first rainy day!

Prefabricated Skylights

Prefabricated plastic bubbles or flat plastic skylights are installed in a different manner than homemade skylights. These units (often called box or bubble skylights) do not require a batten strip around the curb or the aluminum angle. (See Drawing 27.) The units are ready to slip into a curb (the curb consists of 2-×-6-inch boards nailed at the corners and fitted into the roof). The outer perimeter of the box skylight is usually made of aluminum and has merely to be slipped over the wooden curb and attached with nonhardening silicone.

Cutting the opening for a panel-type skylight.

Opening framed for panel-type skylight.

Typical steel and glass A-frame skylight.

Wooden header placement on plastic dome skylight.

To make the skylight completely leakproof, add flashing. Put the flashing strips in place on the roof, curve them against the curb, and then set the box skylight in place with appropriate adhesive. You can use single or double domes. The latter affords better insulation but you can also add a sheet of flexible plastic to the underside of a single dome to provide insulation. Install the flexible plastic so it is 1/2 inch from the existing plastic dome.

Construction Language

Cant strip: Angled strip installed on 2 × 6 curbs.

Caulking: Flexible material to seal seams and joints.

Joists: A ceiling or floor beam usually 2 inches thick used to support floors or ceilings.

Silicone sealant: Special compound sealant for joints.

Struts: 2 × 2 piece of wood to support glazing.

Ceilings | 8

A ceiling need not be a flat, confining surface; with some imagination it can be an integral part of the room's design. For example, exposed rafters and grid ceilings have a certain character, a charm that the more ordinary acoustical surfaces just do not have. Ceilings thus should be decorative as well as functional; alterations can be done easily. I removed my flat kitchen ceiling to expose the gabled roof. Once the ceiling was out—a not very difficult job—the exposed rafters formed a handsome hand-hewed look.

Construction

In this book we are concerned with the remodeling details such as open ceilings with beams and rafters rather than with the actual construction of a roof, but a basic primer of roof construction will help you understand just how everything goes together.

ROOFS

A ceiling (or roof—it might be one and the same, depending on how you look at it) is made up of joists and rafters. (A ceiling can be called the bottom of an upstairs bedroom or the bottom or a roof.) The rafters are set at an angle, reaching from a top ridge plate (the midrib of the skeleton). Ceiling joists (often, 2 × 8s) are placed the width of the roof, two joists spanning the distance from the top plate of the second floor wall to the other wall. Joists are overlapped in the center where a bearing wall occurs.

The ceiling joists are cut at an angle at their ends so they can rest on the rafters and attach easily. Framing the roof is not very difficult, as you will see from our drawings, but there are many styles of roof, which of course affect the inside design: pitched roof, hipped roof, gambrel roof, dormer roof, shed roof, and so on. The construction of these roofs is covered thoroughly in any number of books on home construction; let us briefly consider here the designs themselves. The house roof is really the frame of a structure and as such creates a mood. The roof can be simple or ornate, formal or picturesque, utilitarian or decorative, or a little bit of each. The roofs of the Roman, classical, and Renaissance periods were quite simple, usually flat, and played only a small part in the total appearance of the buildings. On the other hand, the historic French, Flemish, and German roofs were high and steep, decorative, and enhanced with complex dormers and crowns. Without a doubt, the more complex roofs—dormer, gabled, mansard—have the crafted touch, but even the flat roof has its uses.

The *flat* roof is simple, clean, and, for wooden construction, presupposes a light load with short spans or permits a heavy load supported with columns and beams (quite handsome).

The *pitched* roof has two slopes meeting at a ridge parallel to a long axis of the building and triangular gables at the ends.

The *hipped* or *four-sloped* roof consists of slopes equal to each other in pitch; the slopes form hips or intersections bisected by corners and terminate with a ridge or apex at the top.

The *mansard* roof has all sides divided into two slopes, with the lower slope steeper than the upper one. This decorative and ornate roof is quite effective.

The *gambrel* roof is similar to the mansard and is built in the same way. It too is decorative and picturesque.

The popular and effective *gable* roof is easy to construct; it is basically triangular in shape.

The roof outlines your house and thus deserves consideration if you want a distinctive dwelling.

CEILINGS

Ceilings are flat or slightly curved, plain, beamed, or coffered, depending on the materials used and the style of architecture. The flat treatment is perhaps the least effective but the most used; the addition of molding or a cornice where the walls meet the ceiling can give an unusual look to a flat ceiling and break the monotony of a plain clean line. Another way to liven up a flat ceiling is to make it planked. A planked ceiling (usually called tongue in groove) consists of interlocking boards. The boards give a flat ceiling a texture and create a pleasant effect. Finally, you can eliminate much of the blandness of a flat ceiling by using various ceiling tiles—even acoustic tiles have their uses.

The dramatic beamed ceiling is typical of many Renaissance and Gothic structures. Usually the larger beams of wood span the shorter dimension of the room, with the smaller beams at right angles. The beamed ceiling is rigid in construction but flexible in decoration: the beams can be stained, carved, painted, or hand hewed, and the patterns of the beams can vary considerably, each pattern lending a different quality to a room.

The open-timbered ceiling—an English creation—is really another treatment of the beamed ceiling of the Middle Ages. This ceiling is decorative, less complex than the standard beamed ceiling, and is quite effective because the open pattern, like the beamed ceiling, adds dimension and beauty to an area. However, the open-timbered ceiling is not quite as dramatic as the beamed ceiling.

The coffered ceiling has a very complex structure but a stellar look. The ceiling is divided into deep compartments of any desired shape. The effect is highly dramatic, somewhat theatrical.

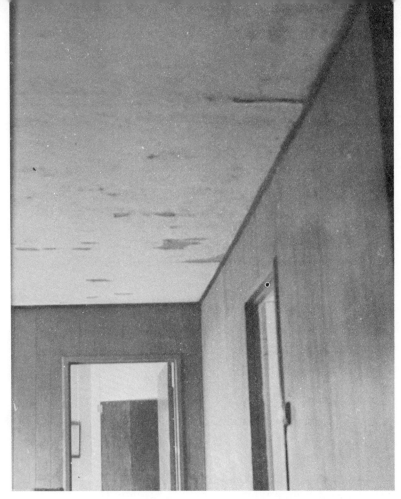

The existing ceiling in the original house badly needed replacement.

The kitchen ceiling before it was replaced.

The new kitchen ceiling.

The new ceiling in the living room being prepared; plasterboard has been installed; this will be taped and plastered and then paint applied.

RAFTERS AND BEAMS

The rafters and beams are the members that hold up the roof or the ceiling. Standard joist construction is used for most ceiling work. Exposing the joists and rafters adds depth and height to a room and imparts a totally different feeling than, say, a flat ceiling. Rafters and beams can be used as a ceiling in many different designs; how they are patterned should be considered if the rafters and beams will be left exposed.

Exposed beamed ceilings are usually made with 4 × 6 or 4 × 8 redwood or cedar timbers, although even pine can be used. If you are going to install a beamed ceiling, the design should emulate actual beam construction. Space the beams evenly or off center, or for a unique look, have one beam across the center, with the other beams butting into it from either side. The joining beams may be flush with the center or form a triangle, that is, be three beams coming to a point. The center beam should always be bigger to create proportion.

The finished ceiling.

Opening Up a Ceiling

① <u>SPECIAL NOTE</u>: EXISTING STRUCTURE MAY BE EXPOSED AS IT IS, OR IT MAY BE SIMPLIFIED BY USING FEWER & STRONGER STRUCTURAL MEMBERS

② BEFORE REMOVING OR REPLACING ANY STRUCTURAL MEMBERS, VERIFY WITH LOCAL BUILDING DEPARTMENT OR WITH A QUALIFIED PROFESSIONAL

<u>EACH SITUATION WILL REQUIRE A SPECIAL SOLUTION</u>

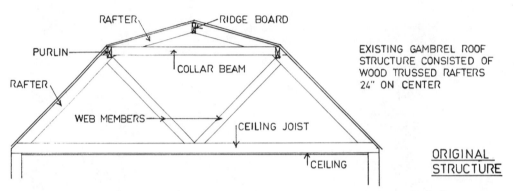

RAFTER   RIDGE BOARD

PURLIN

COLLAR BEAM

RAFTER

WEB MEMBERS

CEILING JOIST

CEILING

EXISTING GAMBREL ROOF STRUCTURE CONSISTED OF WOOD TRUSSED RAFTERS 24" ON CENTER

<u>ORIGINAL STRUCTURE</u>

③ REMOVE CEILING, REMOVE & REPLACE EXISTING STRUCTURAL MEMBERS

④ INSULATE CEILING WITH 6" FIBERGLASS BATTS STAPLED TO RAFTERS

⑤ SHEATH CEILING WITH ½" GYPSUM BOARD; FINISH WITH DRYWALL TAPE & PLASTER

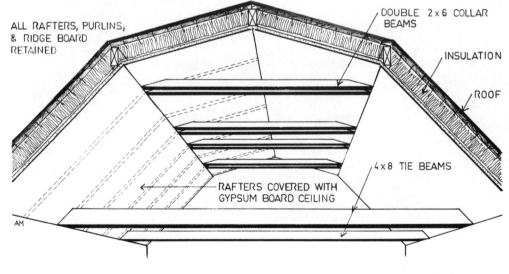

ALL RAFTERS, PURLINS, & RIDGE BOARD RETAINED

DOUBLE 2 x 6 COLLAR BEAMS

INSULATION

ROOF

4 x 8 TIE BEAMS

RAFTERS COVERED WITH GYPSUM BOARD CEILING

AM

If there is an existing ceiling of plaster, adding beams can eliminate the plain look (beams do blend well with plaster), and if the beams are placed strategically, you may not have to repair the plaster cracks that you have been looking at.

Beams can also be arranged on any finished ceiling, including a tiled ceiling. Drawing 28 will show you beam connections and how to make a new ceiling with beams or alter an existing one.

Opening a Ceiling

For our project (see Drawing 28) we replaced my kitchen ceiling, which was the conventional flat ceiling. However, my house has a gambrel roof. We removed the ceiling (which was more mess than work) and found that the existing roof construction was satisfactory—there were collar beams and sufficient bracing. But because we were going to extend the ceiling height 12 feet, we needed some additional planes, to be sure the structural members would support the roof load. We installed 4 × 8 tie beams for both bracing and looks, and stapled fiberglass batts (for insulation) against the existing 2 × 4 framing. Then we installed 1/2-inch plasterboard over the fiberglass insulation, with drywall tape and plaster.

Beamed Ceiling

You can easily install a beamed ceiling in one day. Use 2 × 4 beams for large rooms, thinner ones for smaller rooms. Steps 1 to 4 in Drawing 29 show how simple this construction is.

Prefabricated lightweight beams can be epoxied to existing ceilings, but these beams do not have the character of the homemade beam.

Wood Lath Ceiling

A ceiling with a surface can be very effective, so if you want a distinctive treatment, wood lathing is the solution. This is a time-consuming (but

Adding Beams to a Ceiling

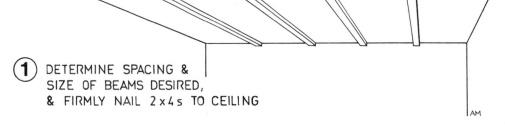

① DETERMINE SPACING & SIZE OF BEAMS DESIRED, & FIRMLY NAIL 2x4s TO CEILING

AM

② BUILD 3-SIDED BOX BEAMS ½" SHORTER THAN SPAN LENGTH; GLUE & NAIL 1" BOARD SIDES TO A 2x4 BOTTOM PIECE. SIDE BEAMS MAY BE SIMULATED BY ATTACHING 1" BOARDS DIRECTLY TO WALLS

CEILING

2x4 TOP PIECE

ROUNDED CORNERS

③ PREFINISH BOX BEAMS; INSTALL BY CAREFULLY EASING OVER 2x4s ON CEILING & ATTACHING WITH FINISHING NAILS

1" BOARDS

NOTE: TO FACILITATE INSTALLATION, ROUND THE TOP INSIDE CORNERS OF THE SIDE BOARDS

2x4 BOTTOM PIECE

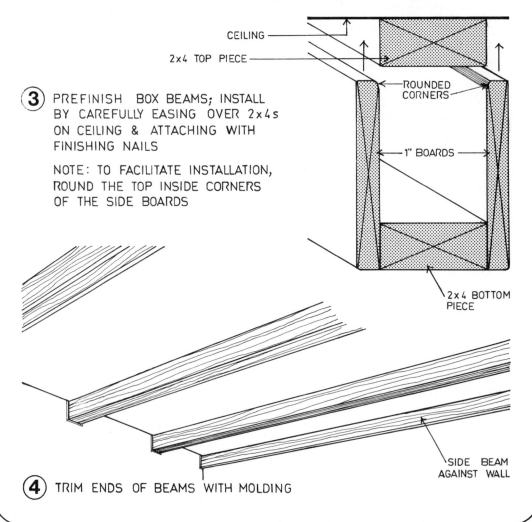

④ TRIM ENDS OF BEAMS WITH MOLDING

SIDE BEAM AGAINST WALL

Wood Lath Ceiling

(1) SHEATH CEILING WITH ½" PLYWOOD NAILED TO CEILING RAFTERS & PAINTED BLACK (SO PLYWOOD WILL NOT SHOW BETWEEN LATH)

STAGGER PLYWOOD JOINTS

SOME ENDS WILL VARY IN DIRECTION OF CUT

45°

(2) USE WEATHERED OR NEW LATH; CUT BOTH ENDS AT 45°

    A. FOR SINGLE 45° PATTERN, USE VARIOUS LENGTHS

    B. FOR HERRINGBONE PATTERN, USE EQUAL LENGTHS

AM

(3) USE A CHALK LINE TO MARK GUIDELINES ON THE CEILING

    A. FOR 45° PATTERN, START AT ONE CORNER & MARK A 45° LINE

    B. FOR HERRINGBONE PATTERN, MARK HORIZONTAL SECTIONS, DEPENDING UPON LATH, THEN MARK 45° LINES FROM OPPOSING CORNERS

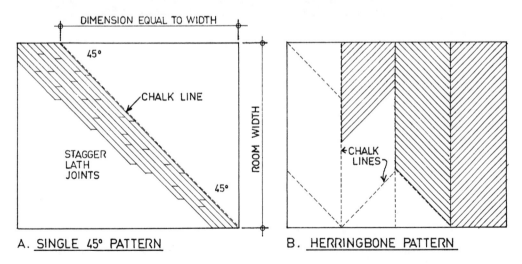

DIMENSION EQUAL TO WIDTH

45°

CHALK LINE

ROOM WIDTH

STAGGER LATH JOINTS

45°

A. <u>SINGLE 45° PATTERN</u>

CHALK LINES

B. <u>HERRINGBONE PATTERN</u>

(4) STARTING AT THE CORNER ALONG THE CHALK LINE, STAPLE THE LATH, USING A HEAVY-DUTY STAPLE GUN WITH NARROW STAPLES

DRAWING 30

The completed living room, ceiling and all.

Vaulted Hardboard Ceiling

NOTE: HARDBOARD IS AVAILABLE IN 4' (USUAL) OR 5' WIDTHS & LENGTHS OF 4', 6', 8', 12', 16', & 18'. USE A STANDARD OR TEMPERED TYPE. PREFINISHED SURFACES ARE AVAILABLE

① DETERMINE THE DIRECTION OF THE VAULTS & ESTABLISH THE SPACING OF SUPPORT BEAMS (THE CURVE & HEIGHT WILL VARY, DEPENDING ON THE SPACING. THE FOLLOWING DIRECTIONS ARE BASED ON A 4' MODULE USING 4' WIDE HARDBOARD)

② PREASSEMBLE SUPPORT BEAMS, USING 2x8's WITH CHAMFERED 2x2's ON EITHER SIDE & A 4½" WIDE BOARD AT THE BOTTOM; NAIL PIECES TOGETHER

③ CAREFULLY MEASURE & LOCATE PAIRS OF 2" L-BRACKETS (4' APART MAXIMUM). USE SCREWS OR TOGGLE BOLTS

④ HOLD THE SUPPORT BEAMS IN PLACE, MARK THE LOWER HOLES, THEN PREDRILL HOLES IN 2x8 s, INSTALL THE SUPPORT BEAMS WITH BOLTS THROUGH THE BRACKETS

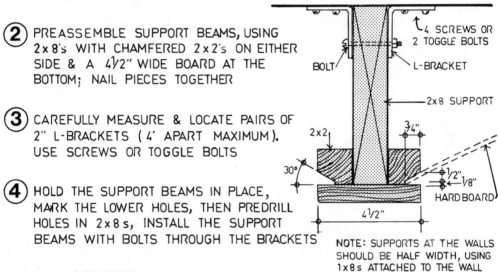

NOTE: SUPPORTS AT THE WALLS SHOULD BE HALF WIDTH, USING 1x8 s ATTACHED TO THE WALL

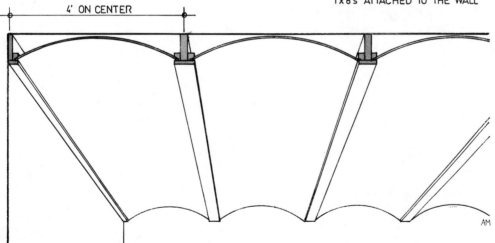

⑤ INSTALL ⅛" HARDBOARD PANELS ONE SIDE AT A TIME. NAIL TO THE SUPPORTS WITH FINISHING NAILS; USE A SPACKLING OR JOINT COMPOUND TO SEAL ALL JOINTS; SAND & PAINT

This ceiling relies on rafters for its charm; note the gambrel-type ro

Close-up of rafter installation.

Insulating Ceilings

(1) TYPES OF INSULATION

(A) BATT OR BLANKET: WOOD FIBERS, GLASS OR MINERAL WOOL (FIBERGLASS) MAY BE FACED OR ENCLOSED BY PAPER OR ALUMINUM & IS AVAILABLE WITH A VAPOR BARRIER
USUAL SIZES: 3½"(WALLS) OR 6" THICK (CEILINGS), 15" OR 23" WIDE & 4' (BATTS) TO 50' LONG (BLANKETS)

(B) BOARD OR SHEET: WOOD, GLASS OR MINERAL FIBERS (FIBERBOARD), CORK, & FOAMED PLASTICS (STYROFOAM), AVAILABLE WITH VAPOR BARRIERS.
USUAL SIZES: ½" TO 2" THICK & 12" SQUARE TO 4' x 8'

(C) LOOSE FILL: VERMICULITE, PERLITE, GLASS OR MINERAL WOOL, SHREDDED WOOD (NOT RECOMMENDED), & POLYSTYRENE BEADS; POLYETHYLENE SHEETING CAN BE USED AS A VAPOR BARRIER

(2) INSULATING CEILINGS

BATTS OR
BLANKETS

(A) IF THE CEILING JOISTS ARE EXPOSED & ACCESSIBLE FROM THE ATTIC, LAY IN BATTS OR BLANKETS, OR POUR IN & RAKE LOOSE FILL OR HAVE IT BLOWN (PROFESSIONALLY) INTO PLACE

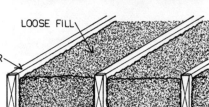

LOOSE FILL

POLYETHYLENE
VAPOR BARRIER

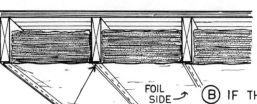

FOIL
SIDE

STAPLE TO
UNDERSIDE
OF JOISTS

(B) IF THE CEILING JOISTS ARE ACCESSIBLE FROM BELOW (BEFORE THE CEILING IS IN-STALLED), STAPLE FACED BATTS OR BLANKETS

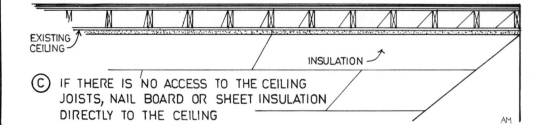

EXISTING
CEILING

INSULATION

(C) IF THERE IS NO ACCESS TO THE CEILING JOISTS, NAIL BOARD OR SHEET INSULATION DIRECTLY TO THE CEILING

AM

inexpensive) project. If your present ceiling is level and smooth, use it as is, although for best results you should sheath the ceiling with 1/2-inch plywood. (See step 1 of Drawing 30.) You can buy laths in bundles of fifty in lengths of 6, 8, or 10 feet (see Chapter I for wood information.) Decide on a lath pattern; our drawing shows the popular single 45-degree angle and herringbone patterns. Cut both ends of the lath at a 45-degree angle. For the single 45-degree pattern use various lengths of lath; for the herringbone pattern, use equal lengths.

Step 3 describes how to make the chalk guidelines. Do the nailing or stapling of the lath as described in step 4 very carefully to establish a perfect pattern.

Vaulted Ceiling

Vaulted ceilings are popular in expensive homes or in churches, but you can have an elegant semivaulted ceiling for little money. (The curve and height of the beams will vary depending on the spacing.) The directions in Drawing 31 are based on a 4-foot module, using 4 feet wide hardboard.

Ceiling Insulation

With today's heating and air conditioning costs, you should insulate your ceilings. As shown in Drawing 32, insulation comes in many forms; the batten type is the easiest for the amateur to install. The batt or blanket fiberglass insulation is sold at suppliers.

If the ceiling joists are exposed and accessible from the attic, all you have to do is lay in batts or other insulation. If you cannot get to the ceiling joists, nail insulation directly to the ceiling, as shown in step 2C of Drawing 32.

Construction Language

Box beams: Beam made from three pieces of wood nailed together.

Chamfered: Angled edge cut in wood.

Collar beams: Two-inch boards connecting opposite roof rafters.

Drywall: Plasterboard in sheets for interior walls.

Gypsum board: A type of plasterboard.

Joint compound: Plasterlike material to cover nail holes.

Purlins: Horizontal member of a roof supporting rafting.

Rafters: A beam that supports the roof.

Spackle: Pastelike plaster material for repairing cracks, etc.

Tie beams: Beams that act as a tie in roof.

Toggle bolts: Metal bolts for plaster walls.

Truss: A set of rafters connecting opposite wall points.

Floors | 9

Floors are the picture canvases of the home, the areas immediately viewed upon entrance. Floors can add to or detract from the total impression, depending on whether they are barren expanses of concrete (hardly aesthetic), carpeting (the easy way out), or wood in various patterns. The crafted look is most apparent in a handsome wood parquet or plank floor, which adds dimension and design to any home. The five projects in this chapter will get you started installing attractive wood floors, but first let us consider floors in detail.

Construction

The basic wooden floor construction is the same for most styles of wood floors; only the type of wood and patterns differ. Wooden floors have joists, headers, bridging, a subfloor, and the flooring material. The joists form the floor's skeleton and are 2 × 6s, 2 × 8s, or 2 × 10s placed on edge, usually on 12- or 16-inch centers. The width depends on the span the joists must bridge. The ends of the joists are supported by either a basement wall or a foundation. If the span is too great for a single joist, a girder is put down the middle of the span; joists run from the walls on both sides to meet the girder, overlapping at the point where they meet. The girder is an 8 × 8 supported at the ends on the foundation; a column, maybe two, supports the girder at the middle.

The floor must take the weight of walls, so the joists must have some support. Wherever there is a joist under a wall, the joist is doubled by spiking together two members. If a wall is parallel to a joist, bridging is used between the two joists. Bridging is usually a 1 × 3 nailed in a cross position to the top of one joist and to the bottom of the joist next to it. Bridging increases the rigidity of the floor by distributing stress up and down the joists laterally.

If joists rest on basement walls or a foundation, headers are used to hold the joists vertically. Headers are 2-inch planks spiked across the ends of the joists. The header is fastened to a sill, which is a wooden member that runs along the top of a masonry wall.

Years ago the subfloor was the floor—the boards were merely nailed to joists. Today floors are plywood (not good for final surfacing) or individual boards. In either case, these members are nailed diagonally across the studs so when flooring is placed on top, no joints coincide and there are no weak spots. Board subflooring is 1 inch thick by 4, 6, or 8 inches wide, square edged or regular tongue-and-groove. Subflooring boards are applied either diagonally or perpendicular to joists. Just how you put in your subfloor will determine the direction the wood finish flooring takes. On a diagonally laid subflooring the flooring can be applied horizontally or perpendicular to joists, but on a perpendicular subflooring the flooring has to be laid at right angles. Be sure subflooring boards end over the joists' end, and use tongue-and-groove boards. If you use tongue-and-groove boards, stagger the joists so no two successive boards are nailed in the same place.

Plywood subflooring comes in several sizes; the size used is dictated by the joist spacing and the type and direction of finish flooring.

The existing kitchen floor—an old linoleum.

Laying the Floor

Once the subfloor is in, you can lay asphalt-impregnated paper (building paper—it lessens noise and cold) across the direction the strips will go down. Use a 3-inch overlap for the paper at the seams.

While there are many materials for floors, wood is still considered the best possible floor for appearance and for durability. Oak is generally the wood used for flooring and comes in strips 2 1/4 inches wide and 25/32 inch thick (widths vary somewhat). Planks are also used in flooring and these are discussed later.

The oak strips are tongue-and-grooved and end matched (this means the ends as well as the long edges are tongued and grooved). Oak flooring is available in several grades from clear to common which has blemishes and some knots. You will also find strip flooring in hard pine and fir but oak has a better look.

Install strip flooring at right angles to the floor joists. Lay the first strip 1/2 inch from the edge of the wall; this space allows for expansion and contraction. Face nail the first strip; use flooring nails that are long enough to go through the subfloor and into the joist by at least an inch. The first strip is nailed through the groove at an angle. When the first strip is down the grooved side of the second strip is forced into the tongue and the tongue of the second strip is nailed in place. Since strips come in various lengths each strip must be completed in one phase; or from wall to wall.

Many times the last strip that goes down must be cut lengthwise (ripped) to fit properly. Again be sure the edge is 1/2 inch from the wall for expansion purposes. Most oak flooring comes unfinished and sanding is necessary to make each strip level with the next strip and to insure a smooth floor.

It is vital that the first strip or board is absolutely straight and parallel to the wall or the line based at the room center. Remember that the entire floor is based on that first row. Always let the tongue of the board lead toward the center of the room.

If you are using 3- or 4-inch boards and want to start at the center line, you can still start at one edge. Here the first strip of flooring must be ripped to the proper width to accommodate the widths of the room and the material.

The kitchen floor with the linoleum removed (see page 107).

As mentioned, use special flooring nails for floors; they are harder and slimmer than regular nails and spiral or ringed for extra holding power. Remember that the nails go into the V where the tongue meets the edge of the strip. Nail at a 45-degree angle.

Always bear in mind that wood expands and contracts with the amount of moisture in the air. Bring in wood strips that are to be installed at least a few weeks before you start work so they will have time to expand or contract in accordance with the humidity in the room.

(For sanding wood floors see: "Refinishing Wood Floors," Page 168.)

Floor in living room being removed.

Wood Plank Floor

This distinctive floor is appropriate for almost any room. Plank flooring is available in various kinds of woods and in different sizes and prefinished, so there are many ways to make a bare floor interesting. Planking is laid almost in the same manner as strip flooring, with a few minor exceptions.

As we show in Drawing 33, you can put the flooring directly on a plywood subfloor, or, if the floor is concrete, put sleepers (2 × 4s) on the concrete over a vapor barrier (paper is available at suppliers). Start with the groove side 1/4 inch from the wall to allow for expansion; surface nail at

Wood Plank Floor

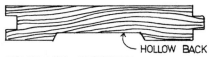

→ HOLLOW BACK

STANDARD PATTERN

NOTE: PLANK FLOORING IS AVAILABLE IN VARIOUS WOODS & SIZES, ALSO PREFINISHED

(STRIP FLOORING IS SIMILAR BUT NARROWER THAN $3\frac{1}{2}$")

(1) FLOORING CAN BE LAID DIRECTLY ON A PLYWOOD OR BOARD SUBFLOOR (A LAYER OF BUILDING PAPER TO MAKE THE FLOOR DRAFT FREE IS OPTIONAL). IF THE FLOOR IS CONCRETE, SLEEPERS MUST BE ATTACHED & A VAPOR BARRIER SHOULD BE USED

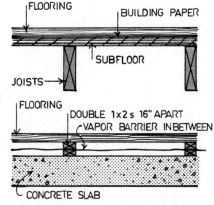

FLOORING — BUILDING PAPER

SUBFLOOR

JOISTS →

FLOORING — DOUBLE 1x2s 16" APART ⌐VAPOR BARRIER IN BETWEEN

└ CONCRETE SLAB

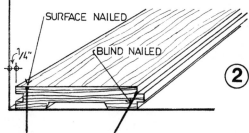

SURFACE NAILED

BLIND NAILED

$\frac{1}{4}$"

(2) STARTING WITH GROOVE SIDE $\frac{1}{4}$" FROM THE WALL TO ALLOW FOR EXPANSION, CARE- FULLY SURFACE NAIL AT THE WALL & BLIND NAIL AT THE TONGUE

(3) ENDS SHOULD BE BLIND NAILED &/OR SCREWED & PLUGGED WITH MATCHING OR CONTRASTING HARDWOOD PLUGS; JOINTS SHOULD BE STAGGERED

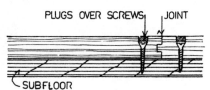

PLUGS OVER SCREWS   JOINT

└ SUBFLOOR

(4) CONTINUE BLIND NAILING BOARDS & USE MATCHING THRESHOLDS AT THE DOORWAYS. LAST BOARDS SHOULD HAVE THE TONGUE PLANED OFF & BE TOP NAILED AT THE WALL EDGE

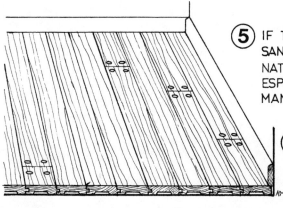

(5) IF THE FLOORING IS NOT PREFINISHED SAND IF REQUIRED, STAIN OR LEAVE IT NATURAL, & USE A CLEAR FINISH MADE ESPECIALLY FOR FLOORS (FOLLOW THE MANUFACTURER'S DIRECTIONS)

(6) INSTALL BASEBOARD $\frac{3}{4}$" WIDE AT THE BOTTOM TO HIDE THE SURFACE NAILED PERIMETER; FINISH TO MATCH THE FLOOR

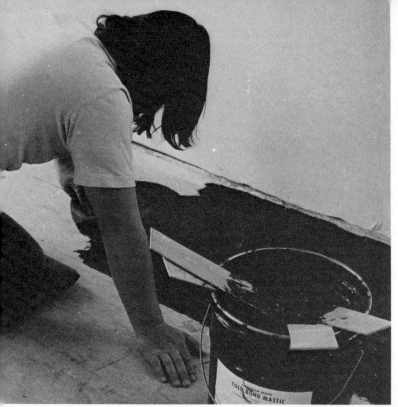

Installing subfloor.

Subfloor installed.

the wall and blind nail at the tongue. Blind nail the ends, and screw and plug them with matching or contrasting hardwood plugs. Stagger joints to create a hand-hewed effect. Blind nail the boards—the last boards should have the tongue planed off and be top nailed at the wall edge.

If the flooring is prefinished, no sanding or stain is required. To my eye the natural look is best, so use a clear finish. Install baseboards.

Parquet Floor

If you want an elegant look, consider a parquet floor. Parquet squares now comes in prefinished or tongue-and-groove styles, with the 12-×-12-inch perhaps the most popular size. Be sure the floor you are going to cover is absolutely level and clean. If it is not level, cover the floor with 3/8-inch plywood with staggered joints. (This may seem an unnecessary expense if there is an existing floor, but it saves headaches later.) Starting along the longest wall, mark a chalk line 12 1/2 inches from the wall (the 1/2 inch is for expansion). (See Drawing 34.) Mark a second line at 90 degrees. Apply the adhesive recommended, being careful not to cover chalk lines. Start at one end, 1/2 inch from the corner, and continue across with squares. Spread the adhesive evenly and smoothly, neither too thick nor too thin. Do one row at a time, and trim the last piece to fit. Clean away any excess adhesive with the solvent suggested by the manufacturer of the adhesive, or the retailer from whom you purchased the material.

Tile Floor

There are three types of ceramic tile to use for flooring: glazed, mosiac, and quarry; pick the one that suits your taste and budget. Follow the eight steps in Drawing 35. If the floor is wood, be sure to install two layers of sheathing with a primer. If the floor is concrete, be sure it is smooth and clean. Measure to find the midpoint of each wall; mark the midpoint with chalk lines. Now lay a row of loose tiles along each chalk line, and use a spacer or template to determine the joint width. Adjust the rows so the end

Installing a Parquet Floor

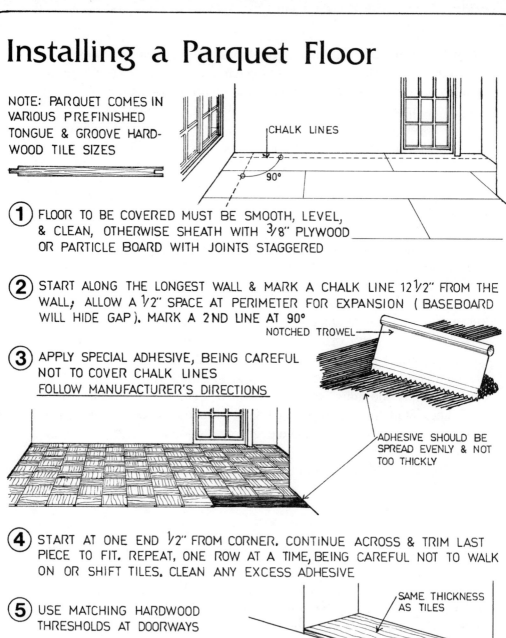

NOTE: PARQUET COMES IN VARIOUS PREFINISHED TONGUE & GROOVE HARD-WOOD TILE SIZES

CHALK LINES

90°

1 FLOOR TO BE COVERED MUST BE SMOOTH, LEVEL, & CLEAN, OTHERWISE SHEATH WITH 3/8" PLYWOOD OR PARTICLE BOARD WITH JOINTS STAGGERED

2 START ALONG THE LONGEST WALL & MARK A CHALK LINE 12 1/2" FROM THE WALL; ALLOW A 1/2" SPACE AT PERIMETER FOR EXPANSION (BASEBOARD WILL HIDE GAP). MARK A 2 ND LINE AT 90°

NOTCHED TROWEL

3 APPLY SPECIAL ADHESIVE, BEING CAREFUL NOT TO COVER CHALK LINES
FOLLOW MANUFACTURER'S DIRECTIONS

ADHESIVE SHOULD BE SPREAD EVENLY & NOT TOO THICKLY

4 START AT ONE END 1/2" FROM CORNER. CONTINUE ACROSS & TRIM LAST PIECE TO FIT. REPEAT, ONE ROW AT A TIME, BEING CAREFUL NOT TO WALK ON OR SHIFT TILES. CLEAN ANY EXCESS ADHESIVE

5 USE MATCHING HARDWOOD THRESHOLDS AT DOORWAYS

SAME THICKNESS AS TILES

6 IF LAST FEW ROWS ARE NOT EASILY ACCESSIBLE, LAY A SHEET OF PLYWOOD ON TOP OF THE TILES TO DISTRIBUTE YOUR WEIGHT & CAREFULLY FINISH THE FLOOR, CUTTING THE LAST ROW TO FIT WITH A 1/2" SPACE AT THE WALL

7 WAIT UNTIL THE FLOOR IS SET BEFORE WALKING ON IT, THEN INSTALL THE BASEBOARD (3/4" WIDE AT THE BOTTOM)

Ceramic Tile Floor

NOTE: GLAZED, MOSAIC, OR QUARRY TILES OR PAVERS MAY BE USED

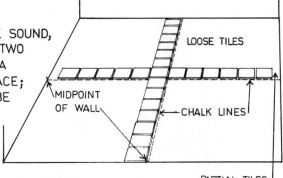

LOOSE TILES

MIDPOINT OF WALL

CHALK LINES

PARTIAL TILES AT PERIMETER

(1) FLOOR STRUCTURE SHOULD BE SOUND, & IF WOOD, IT SHOULD HAVE TWO LAYERS OF SHEATHING, WITH A PRIMER APPLIED TO ITS SURFACE; IF CONCRETE, FLOOR SHOULD BE SMOOTH & CLEAN

(2) MEASURE TO FIND THE MID-POINT OF EACH WALL, & WITH A CHALK LINE, MARK, & FIND THE CENTER

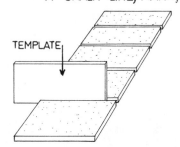

TEMPLATE

(3) LAY A ROW OF LOOSE TILES ALONG A CHALK LINE; USE A TEMPLATE TO DETERMINE THE JOINT WIDTH (A BOARD OF THE RIGHT THICK-NESS). ADJUST ROW SO THAT THE END TILES WILL BE THE SAME WIDTH, & RE-MARK, IF NECESSARY, THE OTHER CHALK LINE SO IT FALLS ALONG A JOINT

(4) REPEAT THE SAME PROCEDURE IN THE OPPOSITE DIRECTION

(5) CUT ANY TILES REQUIRED FOR THE PERIMETER WITH A TILE CUTTER; ANY IRREGULAR CUTS CAN BE MADE WITH TILE NIPPERS

(6) STARTING FROM THE CENTER & WITHOUT COVERING THE CHALK LINES, SPREAD THE TILE ADHESIVE WITH A NOTCHED TROWEL TO ACHIEVE THE PROPER THICKNESS AS RECOMMENDED BY THE MANUFACTURER; WORK IN ONE QUADRANT AT A TIME, & LAY THE TILES, USING THE TEMPLATE TO SPACE THE JOINTS. LAY A SHEET OF PLYWOOD TO WALK OVER THE TILES

(7) AFTER THE TILES ARE SET, FILL THE JOINTS WITH GROUT (POWERED OR PRE-MIXED). FOLLOW THE MANUFACTURER'S DIRECTIONS. SMOOTH WITH A JOINTER, & CLEAN ANY EXCESS

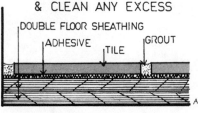

DOUBLE FLOOR SHEATHING

ADHESIVE

TILE

GROUT

FLATTENED END

JOINTER

(8) AFTER THE GROUT HAS SET, CLEAN THE FLOOR THOROUGHLY, APPLY A SEALER IF NECESSARY, & INSTALL THE BASEBOARD

Mastic being applied for parquet floor.

Fitting parquet blocks into place.

Matching parquet blocks for new floor.

tiles will be the same width; re-mark if necessary the other chalk line so it falls along a joint. Repeat the same procedure in the opposite direction.

Starting from the center, and without covering any chalk lines, spread tile adhesive smoothly and evenly with a trowel. Working in one section at a time, lay the tiles, using the spacer to space joints. After the tiles are set, fill in the joints with grout (powdered or premixed). The grouting takes patience and time and is not as easy to put down as it may seem—be careful. After the grout has set, clean the floor thoroughly and apply a sealer.

Refinishing a Wood Floor

If you already have a wood floor you like but which needs some help, refinish it. Rent an electric drum sander (see Drawing 36.) Use a coarse 20-grit paper, and sand with the grain. Maneuver the sander slowly and with equal pressure; it takes strong wrists or the sander will get away from you, leaving small valleys that detract from the floor's beauty. Use a sanding block for sanding corners and along walls. When the first sanding is finished, clean the floor of dust and repeat the procedure, sanding with 40-grit paper. For the final sanding (after cleaning the floor again), use a 100-grit sandpaper. Now thoroughly clean the floor of dust and apply a *stain* with a brush, or use a *clear finish*. (See Drawing 36 for full details.)

There are several clear finishes for floor treatment at suppliers. These protective coatings, which go under various trade names, are easy to apply and more importantly perhaps, easy to maintain. They wear well and offer a fine way to show off wood while protecting the surface.

Elevating a Floor Area

Elevating a portion of an existing floor can beautify a room by breaking up the space and making small spaces seem larger. Once you decide what part of the floor you want to elevate, nail 2 × 4s as shown in step 2 of Drawing 37 and side ledgers; then toenail double 2 × 4s. Make sure all tops of ledgers and girders are level. Use a carpenter's level.

As in step 3, set joists across the girders and ledgers at 16-inch centers. Start from the wall and toenail the joists and ledgers in place. Cover the raised platform with 1/2-inch plywood; cover the plywood with carpeting or any other suitable material.

Wooden Squares

If you do not want to pay for wooden boards or attempt the installation of a wood floor, try the 12 × 12-inch tongue-and-groove squares

The completed floor.

Refinishing a Wood Floor

(1) CLEAR THE ROOM, TAPE ANY DUCTS, & REMOVE THE BASEBOARD. CHECK THE FLOOR BOARDS SO THAT THEY'RE TIGHT, & COUNTERSINK ANY EXPOSED NAILS; FILL HOLES & CRACKS WITH WOOD PUTTY

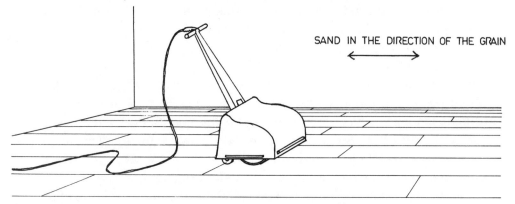

SAND IN THE DIRECTION OF THE GRAIN

(2) USE AN ELECTRIC DRUM SANDER WITH A COARSE 20 GRIT SANDPAPER. PROCEED SLOWLY & SAND WITH THE GRAIN, USE A SANDING BLOCK, A BELT SANDER, OR A DISC SANDER AGAINST THE WALLS

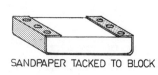

SANDPAPER TACKED TO BLOCK

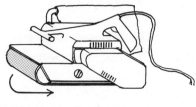

(3) WHEN THE FIRST SANDING IS FINISHED, CLEAN THE FLOOR OF DUST & REPEAT THE SAME PROCEDURE, SANDING WITH A MEDIUM 40 GRIT SANDPAPER

(4) FOR THE FINAL SANDING USE A FINE, 100 GRIT SANDPAPER

BRUSH WITH THE GRAIN

(5) THOROUGHLY CLEAN THE FLOOR OF DUST; LEAVE NATURAL OR APPLY A STAIN WITH A BRUSH (FOLLOW DIRECTIONS ON THE CAN)

AM

(6) APPLY A CLEAR FINISH MADE ESPECIALLY FOR FLOORS (FOLLOW THE MANUFACTURER'S DIRECTIONS). REFINISH THE BASEBOARD TO MATCH & REINSTALL WHEN THE FLOOR IS THROUGHLY DRY. AS A FINAL FINISH USE A SLIP-RESISTANT PASTE WAX & BUFF

Elevating a Floor Area

NOTE: CHECK BUILDING CODES
FOR MINIMUM CEILING HEIGHT OF
RAISED AREA (USUALLY 7'-6")

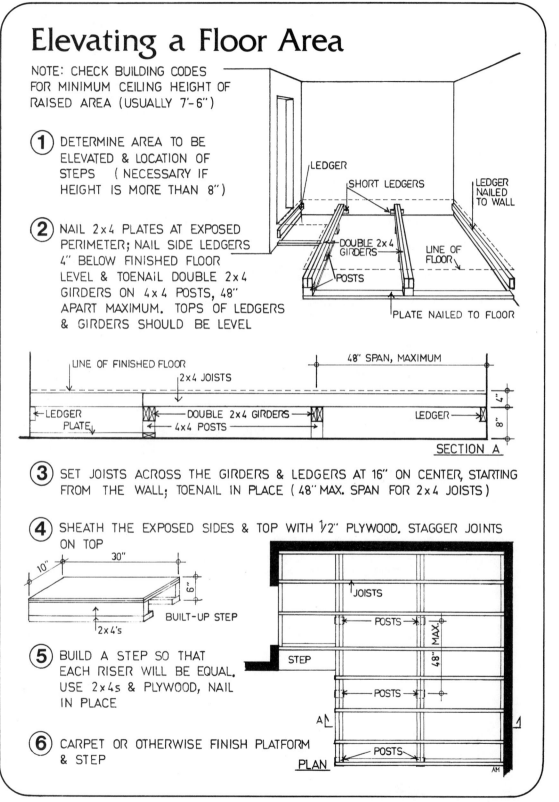

(1) DETERMINE AREA TO BE
ELEVATED & LOCATION OF
STEPS (NECESSARY IF
HEIGHT IS MORE THAN 8")

(2) NAIL 2x4 PLATES AT EXPOSED
PERIMETER; NAIL SIDE LEDGERS
4" BELOW FINISHED FLOOR
LEVEL & TOENAIL DOUBLE 2x4
GIRDERS ON 4x4 POSTS, 48"
APART MAXIMUM. TOPS OF LEDGERS
& GIRDERS SHOULD BE LEVEL

LEDGER

SHORT LEDGERS

LEDGER
NAILED
TO WALL

DOUBLE 2x4
GIRDERS

LINE OF
FLOOR

POSTS

PLATE NAILED TO FLOOR

LINE OF FINISHED FLOOR

2x4 JOISTS

48" SPAN, MAXIMUM

LEDGER
PLATE

DOUBLE 2x4 GIRDERS

4x4 POSTS

LEDGER

4"

8"

SECTION A

(3) SET JOISTS ACROSS THE GIRDERS & LEDGERS AT 16" ON CENTER, STARTING
FROM THE WALL; TOENAIL IN PLACE (48" MAX. SPAN FOR 2x4 JOISTS)

(4) SHEATH THE EXPOSED SIDES & TOP WITH ½" PLYWOOD. STAGGER JOINTS
ON TOP

30"

10"

6"

BUILT-UP STEP

2x4's

JOISTS

POSTS

48" MAX.

STEP

(5) BUILD A STEP SO THAT
EACH RISER WILL BE EQUAL.
USE 2x4s & PLYWOOD, NAIL
IN PLACE

POSTS

A

A

(6) CARPET OR OTHERWISE FINISH PLATFORM
& STEP

POSTS

PLAN

AM

(plain-edge squares do not work well). With squares you can get an interesting checkerboard effect. The woods available run the gamut from exotic cabinet woods to oak and plywood. Installation is a breeze: today many of the squares are self-adhesive, or you can buy adhesive. Avoid the chipboard or hardwood particle squares because they are cheap looking.

Construction Language

Blind-nailed: Nailing through wood so nailheads do not show.

Building paper: Kraft paper used as insulation against moisture.

Grout: Mortar used to fill joints between tile.

Parquet: A patterned floor of an inlay of different geometrical-shaped wood.

Planed: Surfaced and smooth.

Sleepers: A board fixed to a concrete floor to serve as surface for wood.

Subfloor: Rough plywood; on top of this finished floor is laid.

Vapor barrier: Usually aluminum foil or kraft paper to prevent water vapor from penetrating to walls or floor.

Sun-rooms | 10

W hether you call it a sun-room and build it from scratch or reconvert a porch and call it a sun porch or design a solarium, this additional space will make your dwelling handsomer and raise your spirits. It is a happy room for plants and people and creates an old-fashioned ambience that is sadly lacking in contemporary homes.

The sun-room is not new; it was a staple part of the old English house (sometimes also called a sitting room or breakfast room). It breaks the monotony of the typical house plan and creates comfortable additional living space.

In this chapter we discuss building a sun-room to add to your existing dwelling, and converting a porch into a sun-room.

Location and Size

The idea of the sun-room is to place it properly so it benefits from the rays of the sun, a comfort on chilly autumn mornings and cold winter afternoons. A southern exposure is what you want but if this isn't possible, then a western exposure is second choice and eastern, third. Let's hypothesize that you do have space on the south side of the house.

Now that the location is determined, what about size? The average sun-room need not be large (indeed it should not be because generally it will then be out of proportion to the rest of the house). A good size (and my sun-room is used as an example) is 10 ×12 or 14 feet. This gives ample space for furniture and seating—and a few plants.

The room can adjoin almost any other room of the house; I have seen lovely sun-rooms next to the kitchen, the living room, and even a bedroom. In any case, it increases the actual footage of the house and further creates an illusion of space.

As a lean-to it also eliminates building a fourth wall and requires only a three-wall construction.

Be careful when designing the enclosed space; do not make it all glass. It will be too hot in summer and too cold in winter. A good idea is to make the south wall 30 percent glass; if you like (but it is not necessary) include top light using skylights (see Chapter VII).

In essence, plan a bit by drawing sketches on paper before you decide on a specific place for the sun-room. Draw a basic floor plan of the house and add the sun-room in several places until you come up with a definite location. Even the roughest sketch will give you some idea of proportion and scale.

Basic Construction

The basic construction of the sun-room requires footings and foundations. This may sound formidable but it is not. The footing is simply a concrete wall or a slab to support the room. The formidable part of the footing is digging out the soil to prepare a level terrain for the pouring of the concrete. This takes time and muscle. You can have the slab or footing poured professionally or tackle it yourself. Size should determine which route to take. You can certainly do a small 8-×-10-foot sun-room. Once the ground is prepared, forms for holding the concrete footing are put in place. (You can rent these at rent-it firms.)

Looking out to where the new sun porch will be.

Footings

Footings and foundations anchor the building in the ground and are your first consideration (a footing is part of the foundation). They are necessary for any type of room and several types of footings are shown in Drawings 38 and 39. Footings vary and may be of slab construction, or a

Adding an Enclosed · · ·

NOTE: BY UTILIZING THE AREA FORMED BY TWO RIGHT ANGLE WALLS, ONLY TWO ADDITIONAL WALLS NEED BE BUILT

① DETERMINE THE LOCATION & SIZE OF THE ROOM; CHECK THE LOCAL BUILDING CODES FOR THE REQUIREMENTS CONCERNING THE CONCRETE SLAB (SIZE OF FOOTINGS, REINFORCING, ETC.) & THE STRUCTURE (TYPES OF MATERIALS, SIZES OF STUDS, POSTS, HEADERS, BEAMS, ETC.)

② CONCRETE SLABS & FOOTINGS SHOULD GENERALLY BE DONE BY PROFESSIONALS THIS IN-CLUDES ACCURATE LAYOUT, EX-CAVATION, FILL (IF REQUIRED), FORMWORK, REINFORCING, & THE POURING & FINISHING OF THE CONCRETE

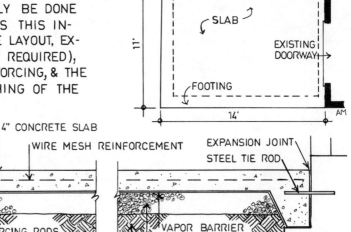

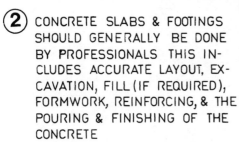

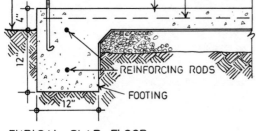

TYPICAL SLAB FLOOR

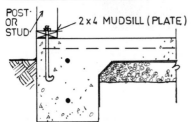

③ ONCE THE CONCRETE IS CURED, ATTACH THE 2 x 4 REDWOOD OR PRESSURE-TREATED MUDSILL TO THE ANCHOR BOLTS (EXCEPT AT DOORWAYS); THE FINISHED SURFACE CAN BE CONCRETE OR BE SURFACED WITH CERAMIC TILE

④ FRAME IN THE NEW WALLS WITH 2 x 4 STUDS & 3 x 4 POSTS BETWEEN THE FIXED GLASS WINDOWS. SET IN A 4 x 6 HEADER ON STUDS OVER THE FRENCH DOOR OPENING. TIE THE WHOLE WITH A DOUBLE 2 x 4 TOP PLATE. THE NEW STRUCTURE SHOULD BE TIED INTO THE EXISTING STRUCTURE WITH LAG SCREWS

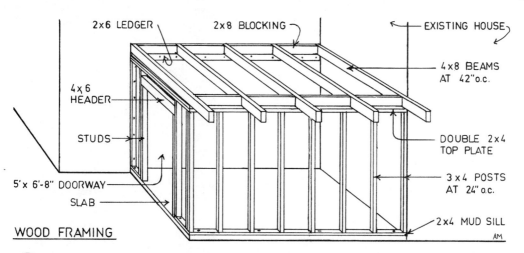

2x6 LEDGER   2x8 BLOCKING   ← EXISTING HOUSE

4x8 BEAMS
AT 42" o.c.

4x6
HEADER

DOUBLE 2x4
TOP PLATE

STUDS →

5' x 6'-8" DOORWAY

SLAB —

3 x 4 POSTS
AT 24" o.c.

2x4 MUD SILL
AM

WOOD FRAMING

⑤ ATTACH A 2x6 LEDGER, WITH LAG SCREWS, TO THE EXISTING HOUSE WALL 2" HIGHER THAN THE OPPOSITE TOP PLATE SO THAT THE ROOF WILL HAVE A SLIGHT SLOPE; SET THE 4x8 BEAMS WITH 2x8 BLOCKING BE- TWEEN AT THE LEDGER & THE TOP PLATE; TOENAIL IN PLACE

⑥ SHEATH THE ROOF WITH 2x6 TONGUE & GROOVE DECKING; LEAVE OPENINGS FOR SKYLIGHTS (SEE <u>OPENING FOR A SKYLIGHT</u>). IT IS ADVISABLE TO HAVE THE BUILT-UP ROOFING PROFESSIONALLY IN- STALLED. BE SURE THAT THERE IS FLASHING WHERE THE ROOF MEETS THE HOUSE WALL

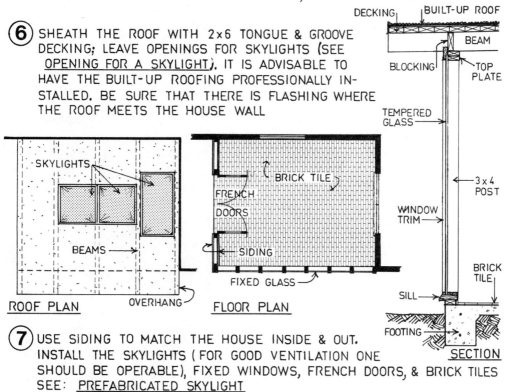

DECKING   BUILT-UP ROOF

BEAM

BLOCKING   TOP
PLATE

TEMPERED
GLASS

3 x 4
POST

WINDOW
TRIM

SKYLIGHTS

BRICK TILE

FRENCH
DOORS

SIDING

BRICK
TILE

BEAMS →

SILL

FIXED GLASS

ROOF PLAN   OVERHANG   **FLOOR PLAN**   FOOTING   **SECTION**

⑦ USE SIDING TO MATCH THE HOUSE INSIDE & OUT. INSTALL THE SKYLIGHTS (FOR GOOD VENTILATION ONE SHOULD BE OPERABLE), FIXED WINDOWS, FRENCH DOORS, & BRICK TILES
SEE: <u>PREFABRICATED SKYLIGHT</u>
<u>WINDOWS</u>
<u>FRENCH DOORS</u>
<u>CERAMIC TILE FLOOR</u>

· · · Sun Porch

Unusual sun porch addition that adjoins a kitchen wall; not a lean-to but a standard type construction addition with emphasis on light. (Photo by Tom C. Clark)

footing-and-foundation wall, or a footing with a masonry wall. Whichever design you follow, excavation of existing soil will be necessary. (Footings may also be concrete tubes or precast piers, sometimes called footings too.)

So although designs may vary depending upon where you live and building codes, the following general plan can be used.

1. Drive twelve stakes 4 to 8 feet from the prospective dividing corners of the desired design. Then, using string, lay out the exact plan of the building from stake to stake.

2. Dig a trench around the desired perimeter of the proposed site. Make the trench approximately 2 feet wide and a minimum of 1 foot deep (or whatever building codes advise).

3. Once you have decided on the height of the foundation, use a level to be certain all stakes are equal. (Note: If possible, leave 3-inch holes in the base of the foundation about every 6 feet so water can run off to a lower grade. The drainpipe should extend all around the exterior of the room at the basef the footing in the trench.)

4. Foundation-framing equipment is usually available on a rental basis. If not, use 3/4-inch plywood to frame the foundation. The width of the footing should be 8 inches (or whatever local building codes require).

5. Reinforce footings with steel rods laid horizontally and vertically within the footing. Pound the vertical rods into the ground between the foundation framing and then, using wires, tie the horizontal rods to the vertical ones.

6. Leave 1/4- to 1/2-inch "D" anchor bolts (available at lumberyards) protruding from the top of the footing so there will be a base to secure the bearing plate. The plate should be laid approximately 1 inch inside the outside line of the footing.

7. Apply a vapor seal to the top of the footing to stop capillary action.

8. Be sure there is an adequate drainage system at the base of and through the foundation or under the slab to carry off excess water.

9. For outside drainage, place drain tiles at the base and through the footings, on 4 to 6 inches of rough gravel.

10. For inside drainage, plan a floor drain (optional). Before the floor is installed, locate the drainage heads in a low area of the flooring.

Concrete Floors

Concrete is an economical and durable floor because it resists water spill if there are plants and it retains heat. Always install a gravel base; this provides a solid level place for concrete to rest and helps to eliminate cracks in the concrete. Over the gravel install a plastic sheet which will act as a vapor barrier.

The floor is poured along with the foundation and should be at least 4 inches thick and reinforced with steel rods and wire mesh. Again, be sure the ground is absolutely level; otherwise concrete can eventually develop cracks.

Foundation for sun porch excavated and tie-rods in place, forms set.

To build a concrete floor you will need wooden forms, that is forms to hold the concrete until it sets. You can build your own forms, but in most parts of the country you can rent them, or steel stake forms, which can also be rented, are even better. The forms must be put in place absolutely level with the top wood board floor-level. Reinforcing steel rods must go around the footing; these support the weight of the building and anchor it.

You can mix your own concrete for a small area (5 × 10 feet) by renting a power mixer and putting in cement, sand, and gravel. The usual proportion is 1 part cement to 2 parts sand to 2 parts gravel or aggregate. Into the mixer put water, then gravel, then sand, finishing with the cement. The job must be done quickly, before drying sets in, and the floor must be smoothed at one time.

For larger areas buy ready-mixed concrete and have it delivered to the site. A truck generally holds about 7 yards; the concrete runs from the chute directly into the site where you have the forms in place. (You can also have companies pump concrete up a hill or into inaccessible places, but that will of course cost more money.) Ready-mixed concrete is a boon, but you must be prepared to work fast, within a 30-minute period, or you will get charged overtime. Try to have three men on hand; one to guide the chute (or the truck driver might do this), and two men with floats and trowels to get the mix in place. If concrete starts to set before you have finished the pour, you are in trouble, so keep working, and fast. As the pour is being done, take sticks and poke into the footings to be sure concrete gets to all voids in trenches.

Distributing the concrete at a uniform level in the form area is known as screeding. This is done with a screed board (two pieces of wood nailed to each other—a 2 × 4 with a 1 × 2 handle). Use the screed board (and wear rubber boots) to level the concrete as it is poured; push and pull the board to achieve the level surface. Keep a flat-nosed shovel on hand if the pouring gets ahead of you and too much concrete is dumped at one time. Next, tamp down the concrete (this step can be omitted); run an expanded metal screen over the concrete to level the slab and bring water, sand, and cement to the surface. Use a float (a 2 × 6 wooden board with a handle) to further level the concrete. Work it over large areas while the concrete is still wet. Do not dig it in; use a light touch. Be sure the handle of the float is long enough to reach the middle of the area of the slab from the outer

A simple wood frame skylight.

edge. Use the float again when the concrete is sugary or somewhat set, and work in wide sweeps to level the slab.

Steel troweling is the final step; this seals and waterproofs the slab and gets rid of minor defects. When the concrete is set (time depends on climate and type of pour), remove the wooden forms. For a few days, especially if the weather is hot, cover the area with plastic or burlap, keep the concrete sprinkled with water so it cures slowly to give you a strong floor.

Brick also makes a handsome floor; it has a hand-hewn look and adds charm to an area. A brick floor is also impervious to water—this is especially helpful where the area has many plants—and makes the room cosier than slab concrete floors.

Walls

Wall construction generally involves a combination of glass along with wood, aluminum, or masonry as its supporting element. South walls will require more glass than the other walls. Indeed, it is best to use as little glass as possible in east and west walls. North walls are generally the fourth house wall. Just how large your windows should be depends on the size of the walls. In many cases, long vertical spans of glass to admit light are quite handsome in combination with masonry. Stock-size aluminum or wooden windows can also be used but the total effect is less handsome.

Converting a Porch

An existing porch can easily become a sun room and actually little extra construction is needed. The basic foundation is already in place so only walls and a roof are necessary. Generally, the structural posts (usually 4 × 4s) are already in place; remove any railing if there is one. Decide on the number of windows and their location; frame the openings as explained in the window chapter. Toenail 2 × 4 studs on each side of the window openings; put in a 2 × 4 soleplate at bottom and a 2 × 4 sill with cripple studs in between them. (See Drawings 40 and 41.) Remember that solid walls need studs every 16 inches on center.

When the framing of the openings is completed apply appropriate exterior material that matches or contrasts pleasantly with the rest of the house. Nail in place and finish accordingly. You may want to install flashing along the roof line. Finish the interior walls using proper insulation and fiberboard; tape and paint.

There may be an existing roof on the porch which you can use as is. If you have to replace the roof (some porch roofs are open) follow skylight directions as explained in Chapter VII.

Glass and Glazing

Because the sun porch is built with some glass, it is wise to know something about the material. Thermopane glass is highly recommended, to conserve as much heat as possible in winter. This is two pieces of glass hermetically sealed, with an air space in between. These units come in clear glass in thicknesses of 1/8 inch, 1/4 inch, and so on or in patterned glass in different thicknesses. Thermopane is available in standard sizes ranging from 16 × 20 to very large sizes; and before you start to design or build, it is wise to have a list of the standard thermopane sizes. Custom units made to size are 25 to 40 percent higher and take much more time to get than standard stock sizes.

Glass is available as 1/8 inch or 3/16 crystal quality. This is a rolled glass, which means it will have some waves, but this is not objectionable in small sizes. In large sizes it is better to use 1/4-inch polished plate glass. This glass is polished on both sides to prevent waviness and presents a clear image when you look through it.

When using wood frames for glass (as most often is the case) be sure the wooden members are rabbetted to accommodate the thickness of the glass. This should be one-piece construction and not two separate pieces of wood. Glass is set into the rabbett (generally 1/4-inch deep), and then putty is installed. This type of glazing virtually assures a seal-tight window.

Converting a Porch · · ·

NOTE: BEFORE ENCLOSING AN EXISTING PORCH, CONSULT YOUR LOCAL BUILDING DEPARTMENT

OLD WINDOWS CAN BE USED TO ENCLOSE THE PORCH; AS MANY AS POSSIBLE SHOULD BE OPERABLE FOR GOOD VENTILATION

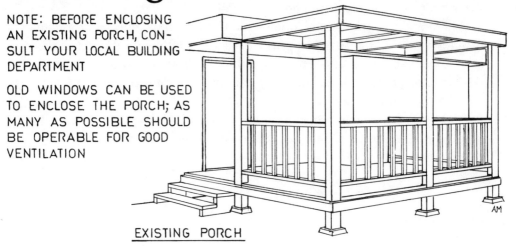

EXISTING PORCH

(1) REMOVE THE EXISTING RAILINGS, BUT DO NOT REMOVE ANY STRUCTURAL POSTS; IF ANY DIAGONAL BRACES AT THE TOP OF THE POSTS ARE TO BE REMOVED, THEY SHOULD BE REPLACED WITH STEEL TIE STRAPS

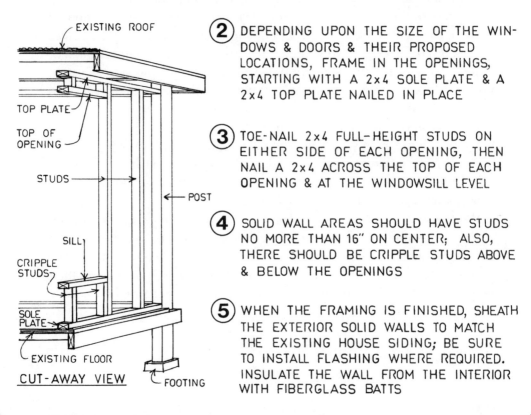

EXISTING ROOF

TOP PLATE

TOP OF OPENING

STUDS

POST

SILL

CRIPPLE STUDS

SOLE PLATE

EXISTING FLOOR

FOOTING

CUT-AWAY VIEW

(2) DEPENDING UPON THE SIZE OF THE WINDOWS & DOORS & THEIR PROPOSED LOCATIONS, FRAME IN THE OPENINGS, STARTING WITH A 2x4 SOLE PLATE & A 2x4 TOP PLATE NAILED IN PLACE

(3) TOE-NAIL 2x4 FULL-HEIGHT STUDS ON EITHER SIDE OF EACH OPENING, THEN NAIL A 2x4 ACROSS THE TOP OF EACH OPENING & AT THE WINDOWSILL LEVEL

(4) SOLID WALL AREAS SHOULD HAVE STUDS NO MORE THAN 16" ON CENTER; ALSO, THERE SHOULD BE CRIPPLE STUDS ABOVE & BELOW THE OPENINGS

(5) WHEN THE FRAMING IS FINISHED, SHEATH THE EXTERIOR SOLID WALLS TO MATCH THE EXISTING HOUSE SIDING; BE SURE TO INSTALL FLASHING WHERE REQUIRED. INSULATE THE WALL FROM THE INTERIOR WITH FIBERGLASS BATTS

6 INSTALL BOTH THE FIXED & OPERABLE WINDOWS (SEE _HOW TO REPLACE A WINDOW_). THEN HANG THE DOORS (SEE FRENCH DOORS) BE SURE TO WEATHERSTRIP BOTH THE WINDOWS & THE DOORS

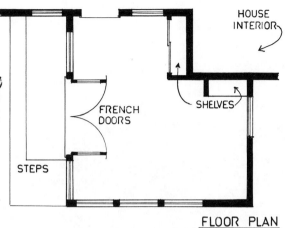

HOUSE INTERIOR

FRENCH DOORS

SHELVES

STEPS

FLOOR PLAN

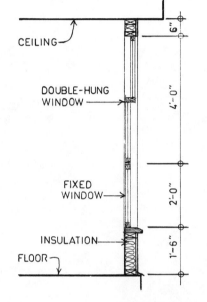

CEILING

DOUBLE-HUNG WINDOW

FIXED WINDOW

INSULATION

FLOOR

6"

4'-0"

2'-0"

1'-6"

7 SHEATH THE INTERIOR WALLS WITH WOOD OR GYPSUM BOARD; IF THE CEILING JOISTS ARE EXPOSED, INSULATE WITH FIBERGLASS BATTS, THEN SHEATH THE CEILING

8 RELOCATE ANY STEPS IF NECESSARY, OR CONSTRUCT NEW ONES OF REDWOOD. ADD A TRELLIS, IF DESIRED. SEE BUILDING AN ENTRY DECK & PERGOLA

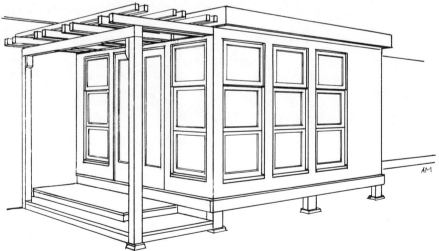

· · · into a Sun Room

Here a sun porch adjoins a greenhouse. (Photo by Aluminum Greenhouses, Inc.)

Roofing

The roof is one of the more important parts of a sun-room. Its design may be gabled, A-frame, vaulted, sawtooth or simply at a 45-degree angle (against a house wall). The roof should contain at least 30 percent glass to admit sufficient light and this may be in the form of skylights or clerestory windows or simply domes.

Glass in metal or iron frames is frequently used but it is rare to find a completely leakproof unit. Clerestory windows seem a better solution because they are set like ordinary windows and should not leak. Flat glass set in wooden panels is yet another way to approach roof design but these, like peaked or canted skylights, are difficult to build and, further, generally leak water. Plastic domes of many different shapes are available too and seem to be airtight and leakproof.

No matter what you decide to use, wood or metal framing to accommodate the glass or domes is necessary; this in turn must be adequately protected with metal flashing to eliminate the possibility of water seeping into the structure.

In any area where glass is in the ceiling, building codes require the use of tempered or wire glass. This is much more costly than standard window glass. In clerestory windows, double strength or thermopane window glass is generally allowed but to be sure, check with local building offices.

Glass must be put in place properly and this is done with putty or equivalent glazing compounds. The glass sits on the putty and is the cushion for it. To further assure an airtight enclosure, plastic cushioning tape is frequently used.

Domes

Domes are a product of American ingenuity; custom-made skylights with glass are expensive. Premolded acrylic domes for ceilings are generally moderate in price. For example, a 37-x-37-inch clear plastic dome costs about $75. While the clear dome is generally used, opaque or tinted domes are now available also. Because of economy and because domes are as a rule more airproof and leakproof than glass skylights, it pays to investigate this facet of ceiling construction carefully. In many cases, depending on the room, domes can be the answer for admitting light. Two or three moderate-sized domes would be all that would be needed in an average room to give sufficient light.

When people think of these units (which come in various stock sizes) they think of a dome shape but the word is used loosely because domes also come in peak shapes and angular shapes. Each style has a different character and attribute about it and what you use will ultimately depend on the design of the building itself.

Domes are easy to work with since they are set into precut wooden frames and actual installation requires adequate metal flashing to eliminate any possibility of leakage. Again, remember that domes come in stock sizes; these are cheaper and more readily available than custom domes. So when designing your sun room have dome sizes on hand. They are available at most local glass dealers. See Chapter VII on Skylights.

Construction Language

Anchor bolt: Metal spike projecting above concrete.

Concrete slab: Poured concrete used as floor.

Cured: Concrete that is dried for several days.

Gypsum board: Type of plasterboard.

Header: Beam or board to form opening for door or window, etc.

Ledger: A board that supports another piece of lumber.

Mudsill: Bottom plate of wall.

Sheathing: Exterior surface of a wall.

Tie straps: Metal strips to join two boards.

Tongue and groove: A board with tongue in one edge and groove in the other.

Top plate: Horizontal board doubled above door and window.

Inside Woodwork $\Big|$ 11

The inside woodwork is more important than one may think at first glance. Actually, interior trim for windows and doors, ceiling and floors, says a great deal about the total look. Thus, select and construct these details with care. The interior trim also covers any mistakes you may have made.

The interior wookwork can make or break the remodeling you have done, so again let me caution you to take your time and do it right.

Trim

Woodwork is an all encompassing term for trim but basically it involves all trim for floors, windows, doors, and ceilings and skylights. Technically, the trim around doors and windows is called casing and that around floors is the baseboard. Wainscoting is also used in finishing-work to achieve

These old moldings in original house are hardly handsome and add little to the room.

another look. Molding is yet another term for trim and there are an infinite variety of these. Finally, ledges for windows are also a consideration and are happily having a renaissance.

While you can buy many kinds of moldings for casing doors and windows, the simple 1 × 3 or 1 × 4 pine is often used for a neat look. The standard thickness for window and door trim is 11/16 inch molding, but 2- or 3-inch material can also be used depending on your taste. You must also have a window jamb; this is a piece of vertical wood on each side of

Close-up of handsome wood molding.

the window. The standard width of a jamb is 4 1/2 inches: 3 1/2 inches for the stud, plus 1/2 inch each for exterior sheathing and 1/2 inch for interior plasterboard. You would use a wider jamb for a wider wall, say, 6 inches. The extra space includes a plastered wall with lathing. So jambs can vary; the important thing is that the thickness of the jamb corresponds to the total thickness of the wall.

A stool or sill is also part of a window and is notched to fit over the sill and butt up against the bottom sash. The width usually extends an inch or

Interior Moldings

NOTE: NUMEROUS PATTERNS & DIMENSIONS ARE PRODUCED IN A VARIETY OF WOODS, CHECK LOCAL SOURCES OR MANUFACTURERS FOR AVAILABILITY

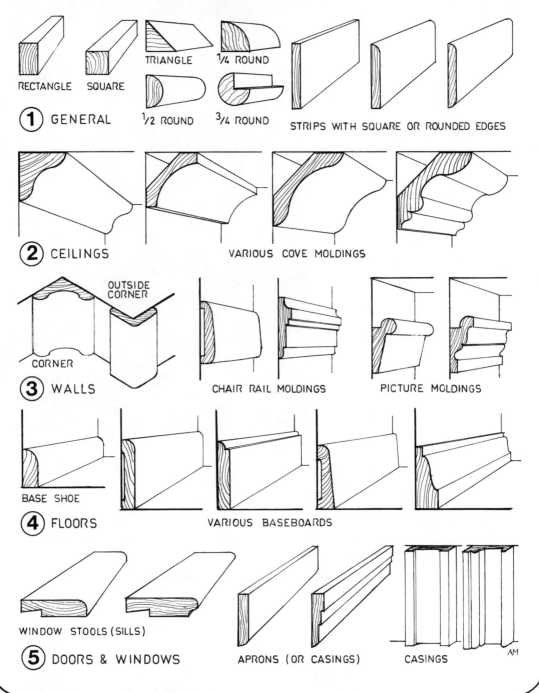

RECTANGLE   SQUARE   TRIANGLE   ¼ ROUND   ½ ROUND   ¾ ROUND

① GENERAL   STRIPS WITH SQUARE OR ROUNDED EDGES

② CEILINGS   VARIOUS COVE MOLDINGS

OUTSIDE CORNER

CORNER

③ WALLS   CHAIR RAIL MOLDINGS   PICTURE MOLDINGS

BASE SHOE

④ FLOORS   VARIOUS BASEBOARDS

WINDOW STOOLS (SILLS)

⑤ DOORS & WINDOWS   APRONS (OR CASINGS)   CASINGS

AM

A very attractive baseboard molding.

so beyond the casing edge. An apron is put under the stool, its length determined by the width of the casing outside to outside.

Of course, different windows call for variation on the general concept—awning and French windows are examples and casement windows also have special treatment. All basically use the same concepts with slight variations.

Any interior door worth its weight has distinct trim and is done in the same manner as the windows; generally doors come with one casing and the thickness of the jamb must correspond to the thickness of the wall.

Floor moldings or trim are of various configurations. (See Drawing 42.) You can use a simple shoe molding or something more distinctive with rounded edges. The baseboard serves as a bumper against furniture and protects the walls from being marred by cleaning appliances. For ceilings

Wainscoting

① DETERMINE THE HEIGHT (USUALLY 5'), MEASURE THE PERIMETER, DEDUCTING FOR DOORWAYS. USE SHEET PANELING (4'x10' PANELS CAN BE CUT IN HALF), OR USE TONGUE & GROOVE BOARDS

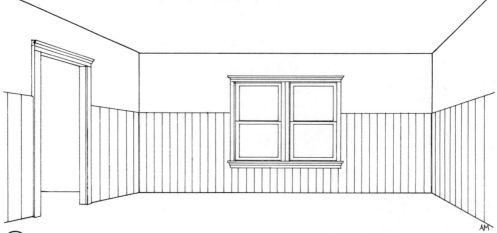

② REMOVE THE EXISTING BASEBOARD, MARK A LEVEL LINE MEASURING DOWN FROM THE CEILING, THEN ATTACH THE PANELING, STARTING AT A CORNER, BY NAILING &/OR GLUING

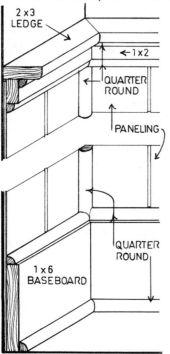

③ CREATE THE TOP MOLDING & LEDGE BY FIRST NAILING A 1x2 STRIP AT THE TOP EDGE OF THE PANELING, THEN A 1x3 ON TOP, WITH THE LOWER EXPOSED EDGE ROUNDED, & FINALLY WITH QUARTER-ROUND MOLDINGS AT THE JOINTS. USE FINISHING NAILS

NOTE: THE TRIM SHOULD BE STAINED OR PAINTED BEFORE INSTALLING; COUNTERSINK THE NAILS & FILL WITH PUTTY, TOUCH UP TO MATCH

④ CREATE THE BASEBOARD WITH A 1x6 NAILED AT THE BOTTOM & TRIMMED WITH QUARTER-ROUND MOLDING ON TOP & AT THE FLOOR

⑤ USE QUARTER-ROUND MOLDING AT THE EXISTING DOOR & WINDOW TRIM & AT THE ROOM CORNERS; OUTSIDE CORNERS CAN BE TRIMMED WITH A HALF & QUARTER-ROUND COMBINED

Ledges

1 LEDGES CAN BE MADE WITH 1"-THICK LUMBER OR 2" (WHICH IS CONSIDERABLY STRONGER), OR PLYWOOD WITH WOOD STRIP TRIM. IF THE LEDGES ARE TO BE USED FOR PLANTS, THEY SHOULD BE RED-WOOD, CEDAR, OR BE TREATED WITH WATERSEALER

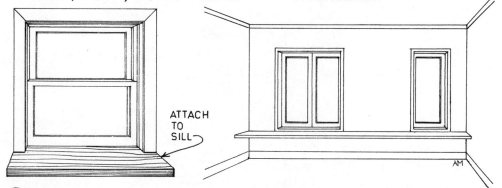

ATTACH TO SILL

2 WINDOW LEDGES CAN BE THE WIDTH OF THE WINDOW OR CAN SPAN THE ENTIRE WALL, SERVING SEVERAL WINDOWS. THEY CAN BE IN-STALLED IN THE INTERIOR OR THE EXTERIOR

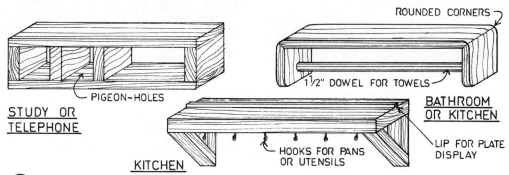

PIGEON-HOLES

STUDY OR TELEPHONE

ROUNDED CORNERS

1 1/2" DOWEL FOR TOWELS

BATHROOM OR KITCHEN

LIP FOR PLATE DISPLAY

KITCHEN

HOOKS FOR PANS OR UTENSILS

3 WALL LEDGES CAN BE AT ANY HEIGHT, SUCH AS SPANNING A WALL ABOVE DOORS & WINDOWS. LEDGES OF ANY WIDTH CAN BE UTILIZED IN ANY ROOM FOR VARIOUS PURPOSES

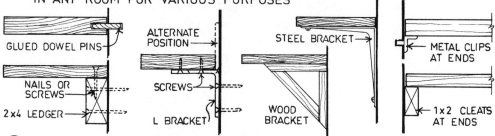

GLUED DOWEL PINS

NAILS OR SCREWS

2 x 4 LEDGER

ALTERNATE POSITION

SCREWS

L BRACKET

STEEL BRACKET

WOOD BRACKET

METAL CLIPS AT ENDS

1 x 2 CLEATS AT ENDS

4 LEDGES CAN BE INSTALLED PERMANENTLY (DOWEL PINS) OR BE RE-MOVABLE (VARIOUS BRACKETS)

Moldings make this small piano alcove seem larger than it is.

there are many kinds of decorative trim; the cove moldings are quite handsome but simpler straight-line moldings can also be used. Your selection depends on the total character of the room and what you are trying to achieve.

Indeed, the variety of moldings for ceilings, walls, floors, doors and windows is so extensive it would be impossible to discuss all of them. In addition, there are general types of trim like square and rectangular, half round, quarter round, and so forth. Selecting trim can be interesting and fascinating so make it fun, not work.

Tiled Countertop

1 THE COUNTERTOP SHOULD BE SMOOTH, SOLID, & LEVEL. A NEW ¾" PLYWOOD TOP CAN REPLACE THE EXISTING TOP—IT SHOULD BE FIRMLY NAILED TO THE BASE

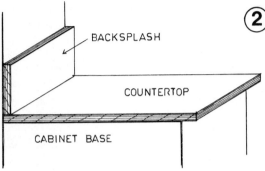

BACKSPLASH

COUNTERTOP

CABINET BASE

2 IF A BACKSPLASH IS DESIRED (ADVISABLE NEAR A SINK), ATTACH A PLYWOOD STRIP TO THE WALL. THE HEIGHT CAN BE A SINGLE-TILE DIMENSION OR IT CAN BE EXTENDED UP TO THE UNDERSIDE OF CABINETS ABOVE

3 DETERMINE THE TILE SPACING BY LAYING THE TILES LOOSELY ON THE TOP, ALLOWING FOR GROUT JOINTS. CUT ANY TILES REQUIRED WITH A TILE CUTTER OR NIPPERS

4 SPREAD THE TILE ADHESIVE EVENLY WITH A NOTCHED TROWEL; LAY THE TILES, KEEPING THE JOINTS EVEN

NOTE: THE TILES CAN BE ADJUSTED BEFORE THE ADHESIVE SETS

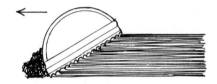

5 WHEN THE ADHESIVE IS SET, NAIL THE WOOD TRIM TO THE EDGE OF THE COUNTERTOP & TO THE TOP EDGE OF THE BACKSPLASH

6 FILL THE JOINTS WITH GROUT (POWDERED OR READY MIXED), SMOOTH WITH A DAMP SPONGE, & CLEAN OFF ANY EXCESS. WHEN THE GROUT IS CURED, APPLY A SEALER TO THE TILES & THE GROUT

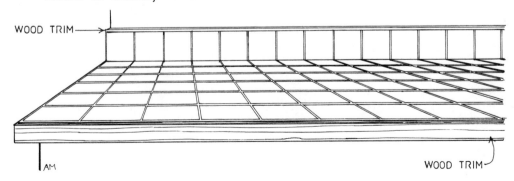

WOOD TRIM

WOOD TRIM

AM

Wainscoting

Wainscoting is a somewhat different trim treatment and is used for decorative effect as well. Wainscoting is applying board or paneling to a wall either to the midpoint or a designated height. It also protects the lower part of the wall from furniture accidentally pushed against it. Wainscoting is usually applied vertically with 1/4-inch paneling placed onto the face of the wall. It can be as high as 4 feet or as low as 2 feet. You can cap the wainscoting with a quarter round molding at top and bottom, if desired. (See Drawing 43.)

So, for a somewhat different effect you might want to use the wainscoting concept; it is decorative and adds the craftsmen's touch to a room.

Ledges

This section on ledges may be a personal whim but I have found ledges of all kinds to be very handsome in a room and to serve many purposes. They can be used in the kitchen for hanging pots and pans, attached to windowsills, as support for telephones, and for various other purposes. They are simple to make, add character to the home, and provide a personal touch. Like pictures on a wall, they add a little something extra. (See Drawing 44.)

Glossary

Anchor bolt: Metal spike projecting above concrete.

Baseboard: Board or milled piece nailed onto wall at floor line. Also called base and mop board.

Base molding: A band that goes on top of a baseboard as decoration.

Base shoe: Quarter round or other type of molding nailed to baseboard where baseboard and floor meet.

Batten: Narrow wood strip to cover joints in vertical boards.

Beam: Heavy horizontal timber or sill supporting floor joists.

Bearing wall: Any wall or partition that supports any load in addition to its own weight.

Bed molding: Molding at the angle between a vertical and horizontal surface, as between eave and exterior wall. Sometimes a simple board called cornice trim.

Benderboard: Thin flexible redwood veneer.

Bevel: Angle cut on piece of wood.

Blind-nailing: Nailing through wood so that the nailhead will not show, such as through the tongue of a tongue-and-grooved board.

Blocking: Small piece of 2-×-4-inch lumber.

Board foot: Measurement of lumber: a piece of wood nominally 1 inch thick, 12 inches long, and 12 inches wide. A 1 × 12 one foot long contains one board foot. A 2 × 12 one foot long contains two board feet.

Box beams: Beam made from three pieces of wood nailed together.

Brace: A board set at an angle to stiffen a stud wall. Usually let in; that is, set in notches in the studs so the surface of both studs and brace are the same.

Bridging: Wood or metal members set between floor and ceiling joists midway in their span. Cross bridging is a term for members installed in the form of an X; solid bridging is the term for nominal 2-inch members the same depth of the joists themselves and nailed at right angles to the joists.

Building paper: Kraft paper used as insulation against moisture.

Butt joint: Where two wood members butt together, end to end or at right angles. The edges of each member are square.

Cant strip: Angled strip installed on 2 × 6 curbs.

Cap: Anything that tops another member. For instance, the top portion of capital of a column, or the top pieces of molding.

Casement windows: Multipaned windows opening in or out.

Casing: Trim for a door or window, nailed to the jamb or wall for a finish.

Caulking: Pliable material, dispensed from a caulking gun containing a cartridge, to seal seams, joints, and cracks, for weatherproofing and waterproofing.

Chamfered: Angled edge cut in wood.

Cleat: Metal hardware usually U shaped applied to wood to support another piece of wood.

Collar beam: Nominal 1- or 2-inch boards connecting opposite roof rafters. Usually spaced every third or fourth rafter, and used to strengthen the rafter system. When collar beams are used for the ceiling under a roof, they are called ceiling joists.

Column: A perpendicular supporting member; also called post or pillar; when made of concrete and a large size, often called a pier.

Concrete slab: Poured concrete used as floor.

Cope, or coping: Method of forming end of molding to follow face of adjacent molding in an inside corner, done instead of mitering if the corner is not 90 degrees. Also called scribing.

Corner bead: Metal strip fitting on an outside corner, then plastered. In drywall construction, nailed over plasterboard and finished with joint compound. A bead also can be made of wood to protect and decorate the outside corner.

Cornice: Boxed structure at the eave line of a roof, consisting of a facia (face of eave) and soffit (horizontal member of the eave).

Counterflashing: Flashing set into brick, usually chimneys, covering shingles and brickwork.

Countersink: To set head of screw or nail at or below surface.

Cripple studs: Vertical 2 × 4s above and below window openings.

Cured: Concrete that is dried for several days.

Dado: A groove cut across a board.

Dormer: A roofed structure covering an opening in a sloping roof, with a vertical wall with one or more windows. Shed dormers have a sloping roof, with one dimension, and are designed to add more space under a roof. "A" or eye dormers are designed primarily for light and ventilation.

Double header: Door or window lintel made from two pieces of lumber, placed upright and nailed together.

Double-hung window: Two sashes installed in vertical grooves that bypass each other when raised or lowered.

Double studs: Double vertical supports.

Drip cap: A wood molding set on top of window and door casings to divert rainwater.

Drywall: Plasterboard in sheets for interior walls.

Flashing: Metal placed where roof meets wall or masonry, and in roof valleys, to weatherproof the joint.

Footing: Concrete platform, wider than the foundation, on which the foundation sits. Installed below the frost line to prevent heaving due to freezing and thawing. Can also support a concrete pier or other types of pillars.

Foundation: Wall, usually of concrete or concrete blocks, that sits on the footing and supports the wooden members of the first floor.

Forms: Wooden members, made of plywood and 2 × 4s, used as retainers for concrete before it sets. Removed after concrete sets. Can be reused.

Framing, platform: System of wood framing in which each floor is built separately as a platform for the walls. Most common construction of wood-framed houses today.

Frost line: Depth to which ground freezes in winter. Ranges from nothing in the deep South to 4 or 5 feet and more in extreme northern areas of the continent. Footings must be placed below the frost line to prevent heaving or movement due to freezing and thawing.

Full-height studs: Vertical 2 × 4 running from floor to ceiling.

Furring: Strips of wood, usually 1 × 2 or 1 × 3, or metal, used to even out a rough wall and as a base for securing a finished wall such as plasterboard, plywood paneling, or boards.

Gable: Roof line at the end of a double-sloped roof, forming a triangle from the peak of the roof to the bottom of each end of the rafters.

Girder: Heavy beam of wood or steel to support floor joists. Generally set into the sill and supported at intermediate points by columns.

Glazing compound: A modern putty used to waterproof panes of glass in a wood frame.

Grade: Surface of the ground.

Groove: A notch running the length of a board, on the edge.

Grout: Mortar, with or without sand, used to fill joints between floor or wall tile.

Gusset: A board connecting rafters butting end to end.

Gypsum board: A type of plasterboard.

Hardboard: Manufactured material, made from wood and having wood characteristics, in 4-×-8-foot sheets and thicknesses of 1/8 and 1/4 inch. Used under resilient tile.

Header: A beam placed at right angles to floor joists to form openings for chimney, stairways, fireplaces, etc. A beam placed as a lintel over door and window openings.

Header joist: A floor joist connecting the ends of regular floor joists and forming part of the perimeter of the floor framing. Opposite of stringer joist.

Hip roof: A roof that slopes up from all four sides of a house, meeting at a point in the center of a short ridge. There are no gables in a hip roof.

I-beam: A steel beam, named for its profile shape, used to support joists in long spans, and as an extra-long header over windows or doors.

Insulation: Thermal insulation is placed in wall cavities, in attic floor spaces, and sometimes in cellar ceilings and between roof rafters to reduce escape of heat. It can be fiberglass, rigid or flexible, mineral wool, urethane or styrene, or any other kind of material that reduces heat loss. Sound insulation is of a similar material, mainly fiberglass, and is designed to reduce transmission of sound through walls, ceilings and floors. Reflective insulation is usually aluminum foil in sheet form, designed to reflect heat back into a room, and to reflect outside heat in hot weather. It is ineffective unless an air space is provided between it and the interior wall. If it is used at all, it should be used with thermal insulation.

Jamb: Side and top frame of a window or door.

Joint: Any space between two components.

Joint compound: A plaster type material, containing a glue, used to cover nailheads and joints in plasterboard wall construction. The joints are also covered with paper tape.

Joist: A floor or ceiling beam a nominal thickness of 2 inches, and a depth of 8, 10, or 12 inches, used in parallel to support a floor or ceiling. Floor joists are set on the sill and on girders; if there is a second floor, they are set on top plates of walls. Ceiling joists are set on top plates, and there is no floor secured to them.

Joist hanger: Metal fastener used to secure the end of a joist directly against the side of a girder or other joist. Also called timber support.

Lag screw: Special screw for plaster installation.

Lap joint: A joint in which one member of a doubled beam or plate overlaps the other member. Most common in wall top plates, made up of 2 × 4s, with a lap joint at each corner.

Ledger: Strip of lumber nailed to a girder or joist onto which other joists are set. Also a heavy strip nailed to a wall as a joist support.

Lintel: Horizontal member supporting the opening above a door or window.

Metal lathing: Grid pattern metal sheet.

Miter joint: A joint made by beveling the ends of the pieces to be joined, usually at a 45-degree angle, to form a 90-degree corner.

Mortar: Material used to hold masonry together, made with Portland cement, sand, and lime.

Mortise: A slot or hole cut into wood to receive the tenon of another piece. The mortise is the female portion of a mortise and tenon joint.

Mudsill: Bottom plate of wall.

Mullion: Vertical divider between two window and (or) door openings.

Muntin: Parts of a window sash frame dividing lights of glass.

Nailing block: A strip of wood attached to a surface to provide means of attaching another member by nailing.

Parquet: A patterned floor of an inlay of different geometrical-shaped wood.

Penny: Measurement of nails, originally English, indicated price per 100. Abbreviated *d*.

Pier: Column of masonry.

Planed: Surfaced and smooth.

Plasterboard: Plaster-type sheeting used as a wall; then taped and plastered.

Plate, sole or floor: Bottom horizontal member of a stud wall, sitting on the subfloor. Top plate: top horizontal member, doubled, of a stud wall, supporting second-floor joists or roof rafters.

Polyethylene vapor barrier: Plastic sheets used to prevent moisture absorption.

Purlins: Horizontal member of a roof supporting rafting.

Rabbet: A groove at the end of a board, going across the grain.

Rafter: A beam, nominally 2 inches thick, supporting the roof. A hip rafter forms a hip of a roof (see hip); a jack rafter is a short rafter connecting a hip rafter with the wall top plate, or a valley rafter with the ridgeboard; a valley rafter forms the valley of a roof, and usually is doubled.

Shake: A thick (split, not sawn) wood shingle, used for rustic siding and normal wood roofing.

Sheathing: Exterior covering of a wall. Used as a base for siding. Sometimes the sheathing and siding are combined, such as plywood grooved to look like board on board or reverse board and batten.

Sheet metal work: Nearly everything made of sheet metal, such as gutters and downspouts and warm-air ducts.

Shims: Tapered pieces of wood, generally shingles, used to close gaps between horizontal and vertical wood spaces, usually along floors and between rough openings for windows and doors and the finish jamb.

Shingles: Siding shingles are wood members sawn to a taper, made generally from red or white cedar and tapered from 1/4 inch at the butt (bottom) to 1/32 inch at the top. Roofing shingles are made of asphalt, metal, slate, etc. Both types are manufactured to standard sizes.

Shiplap: A groove along the side of a board, to allow each board to overlap the other but with their surfaces remaining on the same plane.

Siding: Exterior covering of a wall to keep the weather out and to look good. Various kinds include clapboard, shingle, and board and batten.

Silicone sealant: Special compound sealant for joints.

Sill: Sometimes called sill plate: timber sitting directly on masonry foundation; support for floor joists. In windows, the slanting bottom piece of a window frame, designed to shed water.

Sleeper: A board, nominally 2 inches thick, secured to a concrete floor to act as a base for a wood floor.

Soffit: The underside of a cornice or boxed eave.

Soleplate: Bottom horizontal board, usually 2 × 6 at floor line.

Spackle: Pastelike plaster material for repairing cracks, etc.

Stringer: Support for cross members of openings in a floor. Parallel to joists. Support for stair treads. A stringer joist is the border joist of a floor frame, parallel to intermediate joists. Opposite to a header joist.

Struts: 2 × 2 piece of wood to support glazing.

Stucco: Plasterlike siding made with Portland cement as its base. Applied over metal lath.

Stud: Vertical member in a frame wall. Usually made of 2 × 4 boards.

Subfloor: Rough boards or plywood secured to floor joists, onto which a finish floor is secured.

Threshold: Wood or metal member usually tapered on both sides and used between door bottom and doorsill. Also used between jambs of interior doors; not generally used in new housing. Sometimes the threshold is an integral part of the sill.

Tie beams: Beam that acts as a tie in roof.

Tie rods: Rod used as a connecting member.

Tie straps: Metal strips to join two boards.

Toenailing: Nailing at an angle, connecting one member with another piece perpendicular to it. Opposite of face nailing.

Toggle bolts: Metal bolts for plaster walls.

Tongue-and-grooved: A board with tongue in one edge and groove in the other.

Top plate: Horizontal board doubled; usually 2 × 6 above door and window opening supporting second floor joists or roof rafters.

Tread: Horizontal board in a stairway that is the part of the step that is stepped on.

Trim: Finish material on interior and exterior of a house, but not including interior walls and exterior siding. Also called woodwork.

Truss: A set of rafters connecting opposite wall points.

Vapor barrier: Material, aluminum foil, kraft paper, or polyethylene, designed to prevent passage of water vapor through or into exterior walls. Always placed toward the heated part of the house. Insulation sometimes is made with a vapor barrier. If not, the barrier is secured after insulation is installed.

Weather strip: Any material placed at windows and door seams to prevent passage of air. Usually made of wood or aluminum with a vinyl seal.

Wing wall: Wall built at right angle.

INDEX

Folios in boldface indicate photos; italics, drawings.